Annette Lucile Noble

Uncle Jack's Executors

Annette Lucile Noble

Uncle Jack's Executors

ISBN/EAN: 9783743372979

Manufactured in Europe, USA, Canada, Australia, Japa

Cover: Foto ©ninafisch / pixelio.de

Manufactured and distributed by brebook publishing software (www.brebook.com)

Annette Lucile Noble

Uncle Jack's Executors

Uncle Jack's Executors.

BY

ANNETTE LUCILLE NOBLE.

NEW YORK
G. P. PUTNAM'S SONS
27 AND 29 WEST 23D STREET
1882

COPYRIGHT, 1880,
BY G. P. PUTNAM'S SONS.

PREFACE.

THERE are no murders in this book, no broken hearts, not even one villain. It will keep no one awake o' nights. Lest any lover of what Carlyle calls "astonishing convulsionary literature" should, after reading it, feel defrauded of what he considers a due amount of excitement in fiction, let it be known at first that it is a story of another sort. Of what sort the reader can see for himself.

CONTENTS.

CHAPTER I.
WHAT SHALL WE HAVE FOR DINNER? 1

CHAPTER II.
OF ONE GONE 7

CHAPTER III.
A FAMILY CONSULTATION 13

CHAPTER IV.
HESTER AND THE WIDOW RUGGLES 32

CHAPTER V.
WHICH INTRODUCES A NEW-ENGLAND PERSON . . . 53

CHAPTER VI.
GRANTY TAKES HER "TURN" 64

CONTENTS.

CHAPTER VII.
Aunt Pepperfield's Nieces 76

CHAPTER VIII.
The Letter Aunt Huldah did not get 91

CHAPTER IX.
Jack makes a Friend 99

CHAPTER X.
The Editor of "The Phœnix" 114

CHAPTER XI.
Dorothy and the Photographs 127

CHAPTER XII.
"One of Marion's Sort" 141

CHAPTER XIII.
Part of a Letter from Marion to Hester . . . 153

CHAPTER XIV.
An October Day 161

CHAPTER XV.
What Came of Marion's Ride 168

CONTENTS.

CHAPTER XVI.
GOOD ADVICE NOT TAKEN 182

CHAPTER XVII.
A LETTER FROM HESTER 198

CHAPTER XVIII.
WHOSE ROSE WAS IT? 205

CHAPTER XIX.
A WATCH IN THE NIGHT 215

CHAPTER XX.
"WHAT IS DECREED MUST BE, AND BE THIS SO" . . . 232

CHAPTER XXI.
CROSS-PURPOSES 248

CHAPTER XXII.
TWO YEARS LATER. DOROTHY TO HESTER 277

CHAPTER XXIII.
GRANTY TO AUNT PEPPERFIELD 283

CHAPTER XXIV.
THE LAST OF HESTER PRESCOTT 287

UNCLE JACK'S EXECUTORS.

CHAPTER I.

What shall we have for Dinner?

THERE is always something pathetic about an empty pocket-book; but it was with a sort of aggrieved astonishment that Dorothy Prescott regarded hers. It was a long, flat, worn one, once a man's evidently; but the man had left no money in it, nothing but a sharp lancet with a shell sheath, in one side-pocket. It was there when Dorothy took the book for hers; and she would rather have the memories that ugly little instrument called up than the fattest pocket-book, if she had to choose: however, on this day, she was looking, with disgust and surprise, from it to a man just then passing out of the gate.

"Not a cent that I know of at hand to buy the dinner! and I calculated that there was enough to last until Wednesday," she ejaculated. Then from the front door she ran up stairs, and turned the knob of the first door on the landing.

"Go away!" said another feminine voice. "I can't open it. Mrs. Hopkins is hanging on it!"

"Well, take her off: I must come in," said Dorothy.

There was a moment's delay, and she was admitted into a chamber where her sister Hester was painting photographs. The lady who hung on the door was only being executed in a painless and artistic way.

"It has come to *that!*" said Dorothy vigorously, sliding into a Boston rocking-chair.

"What has?"

"Don't you remember the old woman in the storm at sea? When the captain told her they must trust in the Lord, she said, 'What, has it come to that!' Well, now, it has with us, and things look black and blue. There is nothing good in the house for dinner. There was money enough for a week or more, when an old chap arrived, and asked if we had any children, and how old they were, and, lo and behold, it was a school-tax he was after!"

"I would not have paid it. We do not send Jack to school, and we are too old to go ourselves," said Hester.

"They sell people's cows when they refuse," said Dorothy meditatively; "but we haven't any."

"Then, by paying," returned her sister, rubbing drying-oil into Mrs. Hopkins's cheeks, "it may be you have prevented our getting rid of Old Mortality. That horse will eat us into the poor-house. They might have levied on him, and I would have thanked them."

Dorothy's gaze wandered back to the pocket-book. Hester muttered, "Why could not the woman have had a proper nose?—such a lump as this;" and, drying off the oil, she laid on a delicate mixture of red, white, and yellow, as the basis of Mrs. Hopkins's complexion.

"Tell me where your dinner is coming from to-day, not to speak of to-morrow," persisted Dorothy. "Granty wants chops. She remarked, moreover, quite pointedly, 'that your uncle was always a liberal provider.'"

The artist stopped painting, her palette on her thumb, her clear gray eyes reflectively turned toward the bit of sky seen through the window. She spoke at last, but not poetically: "Do you remember the great platters of meat he used to order for breakfast, —big pieces always thrown to dogs and cats,— roasts and poultry always for dinners, and cold meat for supper? There must have been waste: taking it along with the bills he never collected, it is no wonder he did not leave us rich."

"Well, I am glad, anyway, that every thing I have ever known has been on a generous scale, whatever comes now. We had journeys and parties, plenty to give away: no lack anywhere while it lasted. Think of old Mr. Miles, who choked the parlor gas-burners with fine wire, and made the family drink dried pease for coffee, that he might leave a million. But what about the platter to-day and to-morrow?" she persisted.

"To-morrow and to-morrow," quoted Hester, dab-dabbing at the picture tacked on the door. It was in a distressing second stage of creation, every feature of a different hue, and she had no care for much beyond it just then.

Dorothy, as she sat waiting, was a shapely, comfortable-looking "girl." We do not mean a young girl, and we do not mean a *very* old girl, but just the nice medium. She had good, white teeth, plenty of brown hair, shrewd eyes, and a jovial voice. Her sister was a trifle younger, taller, more colorless, her face suggesting a cameo-cut Diana in the sunlight. This dull day, with a drab painting-dress on, she was plain. When she went to tea-parties, with lace around her neck, and flowers in her hair, people asked why she was not handsome, if they failed to see that she was something finer.

"I do not feel poor-folksy," said Dorothy as she rocked. "Do you?"

"*No!*" returned Hester,—a fierce *no*. "What in the world should we feel 'poor-folksy' for? Do we owe anybody a cent?"

"Of course not."

"*Poor-folksy!* Why, there is our family coat of arms right over your head, fly-specked with antiquity, a lion on it,—a lion courant, or rampant, or"—

"Flippant," put in Dorothy, and went on: "Nevertheless things are coming to a climax. I will let you alone now; but we must decide upon something to-day."

"Yes," said Hester, lazily studying the shadow under Mrs. Hopkins's nostrils,—"yes. Let us have lobster-salad for dinner."

"Humph!"

"Well, some maccaroni."

"It takes a pound of cheese."

"So it should, to be good. Well, do go away, and let me alone! There is a five-dollar bill in my desk, take that, and to-night we will talk. It may be that Marion will have some new ideas."

Dorothy watched her squeeze carmine out of a silvery tube, then took the money, and put it in the worn book. When she was quite out in the hall, Hester called, "Dorothy?"

"Well?"

"Let us buy a cow!"

"Humph!" was again the only response; but she heard Hester add in a sprightly tone, "Yes, that is a bright idea. We will buy a cow."

CHAPTER II.

Of One Gone.

THAT empty pocket-book, that Dorothy held in her hand, began its career long years before. Its hiding-place was in a vest-pocket of the old doctor's, Dorothy's uncle Prescott. If it had been the sort of a book one could read, it would have revealed all the ins and outs of the man's life, — the man whose heart-beats kept its leather warm; the man who for nearly fifty years drove over the country roads, or walked the shaded old village streets. It could have told you, furthermore, about the people in those homes, — strange stories of old men and women whose bygone lives the world had thought commonplace; recent confidences, too, whispered to the old doctor by maidens who were not yet over blushing or paling at these their own romances. But the pocket-book could not be read, which may have been a good thing after all.

Just in the centre of Meriton stood a sunny, wide-awake house, known to everybody as the "Doctor's."

The big gilt pestle and mortar, once a sign by the front-gate, had been, long before the date of our story, taken down, and the pole wreathed with vines. The house was yellow, with green blinds: it had grotesque wings, and an erratic air of doing what it liked architecturally. There were two towers, draped with woodbine, where the birds had congregated for years. Behind the house were grape-arbors, a lettuce-bed, much grass, sunflowers, asters, marigolds, and blossoming shrubs. In front were a score of fine old apple-trees. The doctor would no more have cut them down in deference to lawn requirements than he would have sent his sturdy farmer patients into his kitchen when they appeared in his parlor. The inmates of the house were the doctor's oldest sister — the nominal head of the house, a little lady of seventy — and his nieces, with a nephew. If one were forced to describe the first-mentioned in one word, that word must be the compound sacred to genius, myriad-minded. To know her was to live with her: to live with her was bewilderment. The three girls were the children of another sister of the doctor's; and next in the scale was the child of a dead sister of the girls. He was a boy of eight years, left to be brought up by the united efforts of the three aunts, one great-aunt, and a great-uncle; and so he was reared in an original, spasmodic, but perfectly well-meant manner. These were the actual members of this family to which you have been so abruptly introduced. One year before, uncle Jack had been there, and then had the household seemed complete. Some men are sent into the world to be big brothers to all other people; and such men ought to be doctors. This man was skilled in medicine and surgery; but his uproarious laugh did for his patients as much good as his powders. The way he tossed their babies, and enjoyed their doughnuts; the beaming, old face, and the tender, great hands, he brought into sick-chambers; the advice about that daughter, and the patience he recommended toward that wild son, — why, it all went along with the genuine man; and so love and warmth and welcome almost made palatable his potions, and painless his surgery.

When he came home, the girls had ready, if it were winter, a roaring fire in his office, a generous table to cheer him; and, before he had fairly thawed the ice off his beard, they were filling his ears with their fun, their sense or nonsense. It was a story of the sewing-society last night, or the tableaux for next week, or perhaps a new novel, at which he would "pooh-pooh" scornfully. Did they not twit him then of the time he sat up until two in the morning to read one they left as a trap? All this went on for years and years. The little girls, who had squeezed behind his back and between his legs to get rides in his gig, crept into womanhood, and never thought but that the old gig they had outgrown would roll to and from the door a quarter of a century longer. But one day uncle Jack said he was tired, and laid himself down. It almost seemed as if he had planned to take one long, sweet holiday : holy-days they were to the girls a little later. Soon the people he did not go to see began to come to him. It was spring, and all the doors and windows were open. Dorothy would scarcely be up in the morning before they would come ; singly at first, with a message or an excuse ; then in groups, as if glad of a chance to pet the old man, who they knew would like it in spite of the fun he might turn against them. The sun shone, and the birds rioted. Friends brought flowers and fruit, and came oftener and from longer distances, until wonder fell on the girls why so many went away subdued and silent, or took that time to detain them at the door or in porches to tell them, " He seems just like a father to our folks, you know ; " or, " I never will forget him — that time mother died — if it had not been for what he did " —

Meanwhile the doctor was very gentle, and had time to think of "that door your aunt wants mended," and that old Mrs. Jones's bill must never be sent in, "because she has had bad luck." There was time to have Marion read him the newspapers, and to watch them all, busy here and there; while he let Jack, the wee boy of his heart, snuggle into the pillows behind his back, and smooth his silky, silvery hair. He told Jack how to make a man of himself by and by; and got his scratchy little autograph signed to a gayly-painted temperance card, that Jack might never be a drunkard.

Still the people came, scores and scores of them, and brother-doctors also, who began to sit apart by themselves, and to talk so ambiguously, that Hester grew nervously alarmed. But the warm-hearted friends, and the children that thronged the place, the flowers and the gifts of those golden spring days, filled the house with a strange, heavenly atmosphere, — strange, yet in some way so intensely natural, so like uncle Jack, that when he said quite calmly one morning that he was dying, and had known for six weeks that death was coming, they went on in the same spirit. They let him say, quietly, tender last words, and heard them as softly, watching by him all together. One morning he talked while the words would come, followed them longer with his dimming eyes. The sunshine from the east flooded the bed with glory. Little Jack, choking with grief, held the precious gray head close to his breast; and outside the door a footsore charity patient, come too late, sobbed, "Dear old father — everybody's father! And now he has gone!"

Yes, it could be said, "He died worth so *many*. To *much*, the proper word is money; to many, friends." The pocket-book that fell to Dorothy was as good as empty; but, as things were, she would not have had it otherwise.

CHAPTER III.

A Family Consultation.

SUPPER was ready, and nobody came but Jack. He clattered a jig around the cosey room on the dark wood floor, poked the blazing fire between the brass andirons, seized the gray cat, who was lolling like a sleek seal on the bright rug, and kissed her rapturously. So affectionate was this boy at times, though he was sweet to his aunts only when he was lonesomely pious late at night. He was helping himself to cake when Marion entered. She was slighter and younger than the other sisters, was Jack's oracle. He told his friends emphatically that she did not tell all she knew. In a moment Granty and the two girls arrived. There were to Jack so many "aunties" here, that he had led them all into the trick of calling the one great-aunt "Granty." She was a trim little dame, with white hair and keen black eyes. Her impulses were like the legs of the Wandering Jew, — forever on the go. The girls respected as much as they loved her; but they used to wonder if ever before there had been so much principle, piety, pride, contrariety, kind-hearted, childlike absurdity, sense, good judgment, and genteel cantankerousness, bound up together in the soul of one blue-blooded, dear old Boston person. For, from New England Granty came; and because of New England was the rest of the earth by her tolerated.

The firelight dancing over the table flashed on silver and linen and food in abundance, notwithstanding the publican who had visited Dorothy that morning. Granty folded her little withered hands, Jack bent his funny phiz over his plate, and she asked the blessing. Dorothy poured the tea, and soon several of them were talking at once. This was reprehensible. They sometimes stopped to reprove Jack for interrupting, and were told they did it themselves. Indeed, this family would have affected a stickler for strict etiquette, like a galvanic battery; for there was a freedom of speech, an allowance made for individuality, that was startling. After a while, Granty, beating time rhythmically with her teaspoon in the air, after a fashion of her own, ejaculated, "That poor horse! Dorothy, I'm sure Pete neglects him. And why don't he put the fly-net on when I ride? To-day he kept his ears and tail going, and stopped frequently to kick flies off with his hoofs. Then, again, you mark my words for it, his food is not right, or he would be in better spirits: he acts depressed."

"The men laugh at him," put in Jack: "they say he stuffs himself until he can't waddle. Tom Bates said he would sooner drive a bag of meal."

"Tom Bates!" echoed Granty with dignity and scorn. "That horse once nearly tore Mr. Bolton all to pieces on the railroad-track: that was before your uncle bought him. He was considered a dangerous beast, and he can go fast enough if he wants to."

"What makes him not want to, then?"

"Hush, Jack!" said Hester, she herself suggesting, however, that they drive him on the track thereafter.

"Marion," began Dorothy, "something must be done, or we shall come to a standstill financially."

"We must economize, perhaps. Begin at this big plate of cake: none of us like it."

"I do," expostulated Jack: "I would rather have it than bread and butter."

"Cake?" said Granty. "I would admire to know what we should do if anybody dropped in to tea, and *no* cake. When you have kept house as long as I have, you won't try to be penny-wise."

"What are we going to live on, Granty?" asked Hester placidly, as if it were a good conundrum, that the old lady would be sure not to guess.

"If we take care of what we *have*, we shall do well," she returned. "I heard you to-day, Hester, say that Dr. Woods wished to buy some of your uncle's instruments. Don't you part with them. If I only had now the curious things that ought of right to belong to me yet, how queer they would be considered! My own father was so abundantly foolish as to give an elegant copy, all illustrated, of a book called 'King Solomon's Temple' to the public library in the place where we lived. The boy is having his supper now in the kitchen," she interposed rather disconnectedly. "He looked hungry, so I told the girl to get it right away. I am afraid she won't think to give him pickles: he likes pickles.—Jack, you go and see if he has any."

Jack went, and returned to report that he had two sorts. Every servant and every animal on the place ought to have adored Granty. She lived in perpetual remembrance of them.

"Yes, if you take my advice," said the old lady, coming back to the subject of finance, "you will retrench expenses somewhere. Drop the village paper: it never has any thing in it we do not know already. We might take another city daily instead: I like to keep up with the times. By the way, Marion, what a flat thing that serial is in the —— 'Monthly'! I could write a better story myself."

"Why don't you do it, Granty? I bet it would be huncky! Do!"

"Jack!" said Hester in an awful tone, "I will

wash your tongue with soap and water after tea, if I don't lose sight of you."

"If you do," said he with a smile that was angelic, and a turn that was surprising, "will I be 'Tho' lost to sight, to memory dear'?"

Wee chap as he was, he knew what weapons would conquer the women, and he never forgot a line of poetry. The desultory table-talk ran on until supper was over; then Granty sat down before the fire with her favorite knitting. She made beautiful mats and rugs, adorning the house and consuming wool with equal dexterity and extravagance; or so it appeared to Dorothy, who had begun to look at things so practically that she almost feared she would grow, as Granty said, "penny-wise." The three sisters waited about the room while a servant-girl cleared the table, and left them again together. Marion pulled the window-curtain into graceful folds, and moved two vases into other places on the mantel. She had those eyes that see in a second every thing in a room that can be changed for the better, although it was Hester who was called the artist of the family. She picked a pink flower from one vase, and put it in her hair before she slipped into an antique chair, and looked at Hester, who stood with her hands clasped behind her. Soon she would walk up and down the room, no doubt, quite like a man — would this queer, practical, impractical Hester.

Dorothy opened the meeting by saying, when the girl had gone to the kitchen, "You all know, that when uncle Jack died, taking what was called the estate, we had only enough to live on for about a year, unless we sold the house. We had no idea of that, of course. It is a home for all time, although taxes and repairs cost more than I ever thought possible. We had a great many things laid in that have lasted well, and some bills were paid promptly. I took also a few hundred dollars in notes. Well, the year has gone around, and it is spring again. We have eaten up all the supplies, spent all the money paid in, and now there are only two or three bills more. What are we to do next?"

There was a silence. Jack shot a marble at the sleeping cat's nose; then Granty put in briskly, "As soon as we can turn ourselves, I want a summer-house on that side of the yard, across from the pump: it would save the grape-vine from destruction, and improve the property."

"We must cut off expenses," said Marion, answering the first question. "Suppose we dismiss the girl, sell the horse, and burn kerosene?"

"And eat oatmeal," ventured Hester at random. The word seemed to be the watchword of people who wrote on economy: it fired Granty into instant rebellion. She declared it was fit for nothing but chicken-feed; and, as for kerosene, not a drop of it would she ever have in the house, — the "nasty, dangerous stuff" that it was!

"You are mistaken about the oatmeal, Granty," said Marion. "It is very stylish. In New England, now, they have it every morning. When it is shaped in moulds like jelly, it is exceedingly high-toned."

Granty sniffed ironically.

"As for dismissing the girl," urged Dorothy, "what would the result be? Granty would work herself sick; or you and Hester, who are the only ones to bring in any money, would have no time to paint or write; and nothing would be gained in the end. We *might* sell Old Mortality."

"Good, faithful creature as ever lived," sighed Granty. "I don't begrudge *him* the little he eats; and I should not have been so well this year, if I had not had my little drives occasionally."

Hester's eyes rolled in comical resignation; and she remarked emphatically, "We will not part with Old Mort for his weight in gold."

"Well, then," continued poor Dorothy, "what shall we do when the next two notes are collected and spent?"

"Just this," answered Marion: "Hester and I must work for money, instead of amusement. It is a blessed thing that we both know what we can do, and have done it already. I ran over my account-book to-day, and I was surprised to see how much I had earned in the few years past. Coming by tens, twenties, and so on, I have used it as I liked, but have never really tried to see how far it would go for necessary things."

"I never thought of painting for money, either," said Hester, "until I tried coloring photographs, and some of uncle Jack's patients begged to be 'done in oil.' Mrs. Judge Wilkes has often teased me to paint her a game-piece for her dining-room. I think I will now."

"I do not like the idea at all," remarked Granty. "Mrs. Wilkes has not called on me since your uncle died: she does not know what is proper or polite."

"I have heard that she is out of health," said Dorothy.

"She is able to be out to church, with a feather on her head like an Indian princess," clicked Granty, apparently off the end of her knitting-needles.

"When does the next note come due?" asked Hester.

"Next month," said Marion; "and in the mean time I have thirty dollars for my Easter story."

"I thought you wanted a new dress."

"Well, that will come some way," returned Marion, with the *nonchalance* that had made this family a unique one in the eyes of the neighbors. They never did what was expected of them. Immediately after their uncle's funeral, which was peculiar, although in keeping with the man's life, — no dirges sung, but half-triumphal hymns, and the grave filled with bright-colored flowers, — immediately after it, these girls went about the house in the same garbs, doing the same things, talking of their uncle as if he were gone on a journey. When the neighbors asked little Jack if they were not going to wear mourning, he replied, No, because uncle Jack said that "a house full of women in black was as bad as owning a set of rusty old hearses. It fairly made the sunshine musty, and he would not have it for him." Again, after the first loneliness, the new strangeness of missing their uncle, wore off, they would take life so buoyantly, that it was something for which the community was not prepared, and of which it scarcely approved.

"To sum matters all up, then," said Dorothy, after a long, rambling discussion of ways and means, "we must spend as little, and make as much, as we can, and that is the end of it."

That evening Marion went early to her own room, an enticing nook, always warm and rosy in winter, with books and cushions and ornaments, only in the right places. In summer the birds sang close to the windows, and the apple-blossoms or rose-leaves drifted in, with hints of perfume and beauty. To be sure, the furniture had belonged to Granty when she was a girl, half a century before; but it befitted the abode of this young woman, who also had something dainty and quaint in her person and character.

She let down the curtain, and lifted the desk-lid of an old-time secretary, saying to herself, "I had better take an account of stock, if I am going into literature with bread-and-buttery-malice aforethought." She turned over piles of manuscript, with occasional comments half aloud. "Children's stories, tolerable pay, if good, almost sure to be accepted: I like to write them sometimes."

She opened a drawer labelled *Poetry*. There was nothing *original* there. "Thank heavens! I never was left to attempt that," she ejaculated. "Uncle showed me too early in life the difference between poets and the tribe that would be. I fancy this is the one case when he would not quote his favorite, 'them that are fools, let them exercise their talents.' There are Sunday-school books," she sighed, "always in demand. I could write one a month, pious-y characters, pages well watered with hymns, padded with Scripture; but it is *wicked* work, this writing by the yard, — disgusting work. Then there are sensation serials. There is money there; but, O Tony

Weller! It is *not* 'worth going through so much to get so little,' even if I get scores more dollars than Tony got letters in the alphabet. I can't rack my brains to fancy how a diabolical villain lives and moves, and has his being, day after day; I cannot enjoy sulphur and brimstone that I mix up myself in a pint basin. I made money out of one such story, but it went against the grain. I like to write for every-day people stories of other people like themselves; and, when any thing comes to me as unusually good or beautiful, I wish to say it in the best way natural to me. When I do this, I always seem to sell my articles: so I might as well go on in the old way, only working more diligently."

Some recollection made Marion laugh aloud; and Dorothy, going past her door, came in, asking, "What is the matter?"

"Do you remember my first story?"

"No: what ailed it?"

"I know now, you were away from home," said Marion. "Well, I began when I was fifteen to write a novel that should make me famous. I put in every person, real or ideal, that I liked: I made chapter after chapter, as time went by, writing them on the backs of old letters, and on blank leaves of uncle Jack's 'Congressional Globes.' At last I had a vast amount scribbled; some of it was rather good, some so very *young*, all of it in the crudest shape, — people and plots enough for six novels, and woe enough for one dozen. I fairly revelled in crushed lives and death-beds. One rainy day I copied the first chapter, revising it as I wrote. Suddenly it came to me that it would be great fun to have the whole published as a serial in the village paper, anonymously of course. Then uncle, Granty, and you girls, would read and discuss it, and I, listening, have much sport. I wrote Mr. Sproul, the editor, a letter, offering to send a chapter each week, &c., only he must promise, upon his honor, to keep my secret. The next day he sent me a very charming note. He had heard me very 'favorably mentioned,' 'a niece of uncle Jack's must have talent.' Would I consent to have my manuscript amended according to an editor's ideas of fitness? If I would, he would read the first chapter, judge of it, and, if accepted, would put it immediately into type. Oh, yes! he added, that, although he would be glad to pay me for the story, a country editor could not think of such a thing. It was fun and fame I wanted; and I replied that it was no matter about pay. Two days later, uncle Jack was reading the paper, and gave a little whistle, then began, while my heart beat fast enough to choke me, —

"The public will be pleased to learn that we shall begin next week the first instalment of a brilliant serial by an *accomplished young lady of our own town.*"

"Well, well!" said uncle, "who is going *scooting* up the path of glory this time? I have not been called to any patient with a rush of romance to the brain; but that may be just because she has found relief in this way."

"Oh, I was so provoked! everybody would know what I was doing in less than a week, now eyes and ears were open. I had meant the editor to print it as quietly as he would have begun a reprint of some English novelist's last book, and I expected it to produce just as good an impression, perhaps better. All my enthusiasm turned to disgust. The bare thought of copying week after week, and nobody suprised, nothing but stupid questions! I could not and I would not go on. But that dreadful editor had been so polite! In my pocket, then, was a note sent by his messenger, saying he had set up half one night getting it into nice shape. Would I please not underline almost every sentence, and would I make paragraphs once in a while (he showed me how), and send more copy immediately? they made up their paper several days ahead. But I was bound to write. I had agreed to do it. I had drawn that man of business into a plan of my own proposing. He had even advertised me, which he had no business to do; but thereby he seemed to have me doubly in his awful power. As I had never published a line, it was a little funny that I was so sure everybody would know me for the 'accomplished young lady;' but that I never once doubted. I was awake all night, and early the next morning I confessed to Hester. She calmly said I was a great fool, and would have to go right on being one, if Mr. Sproul held me to it. I declared I should go crazy; and Hester, seeing how wrought up I was, saw also that something must be done. She said again I was a *big, big* fool to have gotten into such a mess, and that I must go and beg off. That I could not do. Why, the very mention of that manuscript made me blush, not to speak of facing a live editor. Hester grew more savage, as she does when she is going to sacrifice herself; and, the crosser she grew, the more I was comforted. She muttered, 'Mr. Sproul is a gentleman, they say. He is an infidel too. I heard once that he said he might be beefsteak in his future state, his body entering into grass, you know, and a cow eat of it.'

"What such a horrid sentiment had to do with my serial, I could not see. But Hester went on, 'Your yarn is long, long, *ever* so long drawn out, isn't it?'

"'He was going to condense it,' I answered meekly.

"'He couldn't; I know he couldn't,' she retorted fiercely. 'And it is pious, isn't it? VERY pious?'

"'Oh, no! not partic'"—

"'I know it is now,' she insisted. 'It naturally would be, brought up as you have been, and I tell you it has *got to be!* Come along now.'

"I picked up my hat (I remember it so well), and followed her down Main Street, until I saw over the old engine-house the sign 'Local Intelligencer:' then I would not go a step farther. Hester growled; but she went on and on, and in. I admired her, as if she had fired a loaded cannon, or started to do so. When she came out, I ran to her, crying, 'Will he let me off, Hester, will he?'

"She declared *she* would not, if she were in his place, and then laughed; and I joined her until I ached, for I knew she had succeeded. She said that he looked politely defiant; said the entire paper for the next issue was made up, and my first chapter covered the whole page. Poor man! he was an invalid too, and he let her know he had taken pains with my manuscript. Hester told him he would have much more trouble to come, if he did publish it; for it was just endless. It went on and on and on. I had been three years at it; and, after a year in print, the climax would be far off. He said, 'Phew, phew! The young lady must condense: it will be valuable practice for her.'

"Hester hinted that it was not adapted to his

paper anyway. He said he thought the first chapter showed talent. Yes, she admitted that; but she thought herself it was better suited to a Sunday-school library. It was pious, very, very pious, more and more as it went on, weaving in sermons, theological discussions, and theories of reform. The poor man grew sad, as well as vexed; but he said, in condensing, all that must be cut out, for it could not go over election. Political matters must largely fill the paper then. Hester caught at that. She made him think the story might stretch from one campaign around to another, if once it got well underway. In short, after Hester had made me out the most completely equipped fool that you ever heard of, the poor man let me off, and said he had the whole paper to make over again. He died of consumption in a year or two, and I feel so sorry when I think what trouble I made him. But I hope he never told anybody."

"What became of the serial?" asked Dorothy.

"After six or seven years I boiled it down, burned up the 'fine' parts, mitigated the affliction, and sold it for two hundred dollars."

"Write another and better one, and get more for it," recommended the practical sister; and Marion assured her she meant to go about something of the kind at once.

"Girls," said a voice behind them; and they turned to see Granty, in fluttering nondescript garments, — "girls, you *must* stop talking. I can hear you; and, if I do not get to sleep when I first go to bed, I do not sleep a wink all night. Dorothy, is the cellar-door fastened?"

"Yes, ma'am."

"And the west windows locked? And the meat for breakfast where the cat cannot get it? And do you know whether the girl left any matches around loose?"

"Every thing is right about the house, Granty."

"Well, go to bed now. If I should not be well enough to be down in the morning, see that the boy gets plenty of sirup on his cakes." Then Granty withdrew to the background, like the little old lady on Swiss clocks; but she re-appeared in a second, saying, "Remind me to-morrow to see if the brine covers the pork in the barrel. Bridget is so careless, it will all be rusty the first thing we know."

She retreated for a time; again she appeared, and this time her tone was quite tragic.

"Marion, if something is not done, the child will be ruined I am afraid."

"What child, Granty?"

"Why, Jack. He says he tied a nail to a string, so it went *tick-tack* against Mr. Bruster's windows, and made him look out to see what the matter was. And, worse than *that*, Sunday I went into the infant department to give him a penny for the collection, and he was not there. That minute he appeared, in a weeping-willow by the window, and looked in. I went after him, and he said he only took that way to see if the teacher was there."

"I will whip him to-morrow if you won't stand any longer in your stockings on the cold floor, Granty."

"I beg of you *don't*, Dorothy. I only wanted to show you, that, in time to come, he *might* need discipline. I hope you are sure about the cellar-door."

Marion locked her desk; Dorothy arose to go; and Granty made a slow but final exit. Peace settled down over the old house. Uncle Jack's great silver watch ticked under Marion's pillow. If she staid awake at night, it always seemed like a companion. It was the same one she had begged to have opened for her in the days when she rode his boot-leg to a song of

"Shoe the horse, and shoe the mare,
And let the little colt go bare."

It was the same watch to whose tick he had many times counted pulses in death-chambers, — he who was now dead. It never seemed to tick in a melancholy way, however, but always seemed to Marion to say, "Make the best of it! Be brave, self-reliant. Do the best you can! Be kind to Granty, and keep well little Jack. God will bless you."

She heard its messages for a while this night, and then they ceased for her. Hours went by. It must have been after midnight, when, as if continuing a conversation, Granty's voice sounded out in the stillness: "And tell her she puts in too much fat, so she had better bake the potatoes hereafter. It might slip my mind; so, while I think of it, I will mention, Dorothy, that old Mrs. Ruggles never will pay the note you spoke of without a fuss. She is a very disagreeable person to have dealings with."

Nobody heard it but Hester. That did not matter. Granty must arise, and speak in the hall when the spirit moved her. She was as unconcerned about her listeners as the muezzin who calls the hour of prayer from the minaret.

"Haven't you slept well, Granty?" came faintly from Hester's room.

"Not a wink."

Nevertheless Hester did not quite believe her. The dear, old lady slept and waked so easily, the girls doubted if she knew about the transition times.

CHAPTER IV.

Hester and the Widow Ruggles.

ONE June morning Dorothy sat in the office, in a huge red wooden chair, before the doctor's old desk. Back of her was his medical library : in front were shelves filled with bottles of every size, shape, and color. On the walls were physiological charts interspersed with bronze medallions. On the top shelf of the desk at which Dorothy sat were three dusty skulls, and behind the door, in a little side-room, hung literally the skeleton in the closet. It had been there for years, always lacking two ribs and one foot. Draughts of air through the place used to sway it, even gently to rattle its bones ; but, these singular young women said, "As we do not know what to do with it, we may as well let it alone:" therefore, undisturbed by its proximity, Dorothy bent over the large account-books at this time, and only shut them to say to herself, "Hester must go to-day."

At that moment Hester appeared, as if in answer to the summons, only she was followed by a little boy with a large bottle. She went directly to an upper shelf, filled the bottle from a larger one, shook the contents, and gave it to the lad, saying, "Tell your mother it is almost gone. She will have to get it from some doctor hereafter."

"Mar says no doctor round here don't know how to fix it right, and she can't live if she don't have this yaller mixter in the spring. She says she bet *you* could make it if you only knowed how."

Hester smiled scornfully, but followed the smile with a sigh. Uncle Jack had been dead a year, but some of his faithful old patients still turned their steps toward that office. Hester often knew what some of them wanted; and, where the case was a simple one, she dealt out the stock of medicine that remained. She had as much knowledge of drugs, and skill in nursing, as many a fledgling doctor has started with. She had been uncle Jack's student, after a fashion, from her babyhood. Granty was one day amazed to find her putting an instrument down a woman's throat, with the coolness of a practised surgeon, and was told, "She came with a chicken-bone in her throat. You would not have had me send her off black in the face, because I hadn't a Latin diploma, would you?"

When the child had gone, Dorothy said, "Hester, can you not go and collect one of the notes? Marion wants to write, and I am busy with Granty, or soon will be."

"What is there to do?"

"To go and find the widow Ruggles, — Mrs. Almira Ruggles. She has a splendid farm; but she always talks poverty, I hear. She is that queer character that told uncle Jack her boy had 'barnacles' all over his lungs. Well, her note is forty-seven dollars, seventy cents, with interest for eleven months. I have forgotten what per cent she pays. Can you compute interest?"

"Of course, of course," said Hester, who, after a boarding-school course of mathematics, was a broken reed to lean upon when exactness was required. "Of course; or *she* can, probably."

"Will you be *very* business-like? Are you afraid to insist that she shall pay every cent?"

"Emerson," remarked Hester grandly, "says that 'a great part of courage is the courage of having done the thing before.' Thus far in my experience as executor of this estate, or, more modestly speaking, *one* of the executors, nobody has paid up to a cent: therefore I have not that courage that would come, had my insisting heretofore done any good; but I will insist all the same."

After a few more questions as to Mrs. Ruggles and her note, Hester opened a glass door into the garden, went down the beaten path to the barn, and called Pete to harness Old Mortality. Suddenly Jack fled over the lettuce-bed from one direction, shouting in alarm, "Get out of the way, aunt Hester;" while Pete, the black boy, came, like a sky-rocket on a horizontal course, from another quarter. In hot pursuit of the latter was an old red nag, working its nostrils, showing its teeth like a vicious puppy, albeit a tremendously big one. Pete went over the garden-fence just in time; then he made futile grabs at the brute, who pranced forward, backed off, kicked up his heels, waltzed hither and yon, apparently keeping up a succession of grimaces at the youth over the fence.

"I can't catch 'im, Miss Hester: t'ain't no use. When I go fer to try, he bites me with one end, an' he kicks me with 'e t'other. He's the cussinest ole thing I ever seed, anyway!"

"I don't think you are kind to him, Peter," said Hester severely. "He never behaved so when uncle Jack was alive — never! He doesn't love you."

Pete had no illusions on that score to dispel; but he only grinned over the top rail, while Jack from the shelter of the pump called, "Pete is afraid of him, and he knows it."

The horse stood like a statue for the next few seconds, then, with a flirt and a rush, charged upon the open barn-door, went through and into his stall; whereupon Pete contrived to get the halter over his head.

"Now, then, do not let him get away from you again, if you cannot manage him," said Hester, following them in out of the sweet June air, and standing in the shadow of the barn. The hay-seed sifted down through the chinks in the floor over her head, and lodged in her brown hair, while the swaying cobwebs tickled her inquisitive nose; and much the small black boy wished she would go into the house, instead of searching into his doings in the way he particularly dreaded. A man might be expected to find out that he had used the chamois-skin for dusting the phaeton as a swab to wash the gig-wheels, and to object to his taking a pound of lard a day from the cellar to grease the wagon; but for a young lady to keep the run of such moral derelictions was trying, and, to his mind, uncalled for.

He watched her nervously as she looked into meal-bins, and tipped water-pails toward the light with her trim foot, that she might see if they were clean. He backed Old Mortality hurriedly into the traces, and sang lustily, "Nobody knows the trouble I feel," lest Hester should see his latest exploit, — the shortening of the tail of that family beast by at least five inches. Happily for him, she went to put on her bonnet before he had to drive him around to the front-gate; and, when she re-appeared there, she did not at once notice the poor creature's reduced circumstances.

Old Mortality had three gaits: the first was a melancholy, dignified stalk; as, for example, when of an afternoon, Granty sat behind him in the phaeton, his four legs seemed stiffened into rods of iron. He paced along, his tail solemnly vibrating, seldom lifting it against a fly, without coming to a full stop, when he swung it around with great *empressement.* To whip him in this mood was to wear out your arm of flesh, and to bestir him as much as if you had tickled Gibraltar with a broom-corn. His second gait was, as Tom Bates hinted, the unambitious wag-wag of a well stuffed meal-bag trying the career of a quadruped: he assumed this in the business carriage. But not one of the doctor's own family had seen an approach to his *third* gait since uncle Jack died. That was a dead secret between Old Mortality and the succession of boys who had the care of him. How they each discovered and transmitted it, we cannot tell; but, if ever one of them found himself away from the haunts of men with this hypocritical old beast, he could rival Brom Bones or Tam o' Shanter as a driver. Hester alone suspected this, and used to attack Mortality with whip, reins, whistles, cluck-clucks, with as forcible language as a lady might use: she never beguiled him out of the wag-wag. At this pace, of course, they went to-day, still with a tranquil mind in Hester; for the familiar country roads were pleasant, as what roads are not when grass is crisp and green, when trees are alive with birds, and over all is a sky so radiant with sun-and-cloud beauty it would fill one with delight, though it arched over a desert? While Hester rode along those roads, it seemed to her she could hear her uncle's genial voice as he told her of the families whose homes they passed. How much he liked his patients, no matter how peculiar they were! He could not shut out of his heart or his help what the tender old philosopher calls "the great world of God's cheerful, fallible men and women," or, as to that, the disconsolate ones.

By and by Hester turned toward an ugly wooden farmhouse, and left Pete with Old Mortality at the big gate. The narrower one, like the front-door, was evidently little used; but she brushed through the tall grass and dandelions around the house, coming then to rickety steps up to a sunny porch in the rear, where a woman was bent over a washtub, — a yellow, inexpressive woman, who stared at her until she understood her errand, and then feebly exclaimed, "Law, now! One of the old doctor's daughters!—oh! niece, is it? Wall, sure enuff, that there bill is doo. I was thinkin' on't last week; but the menfolks is so driv in the fields, that I couldn't nohow git a hoss off work to come in and see you 'bout it. Walk in, an' I'll stop, all suds as I be, if you'll excuse me."

She led Hester through a kitchen into the family room, and left her, while she went for her accounts, her bills, and so on.

"A study of ugliness," thought the amateur artist, left to look around her. "How can a woman who has five dollars not absolutely needed for food or fire live in such a house without making it homelike?"

Dorothy would have been sharpening her wits for business. Hester scowled at the carpet of brown rags patched with yards of a pauper-blue color, saw that the old wooden lounge had a butternut brown shawl for a cover; while a few straw-bottomed chairs, and a bare, big table, completed the furniture. Almanacs, coats, hats, a clock, and a fashion-plate behind a vase of paper roses, adorned the walls at irregular distances. Hester had mentally painted the floor oak, covered the lounge with chintz, got up one unbleached curtain, and was going on to some simple bric-a-brac, when Mrs. Ruggles re-appeared, sat down heavily, and remarked, with a shade of sadness, "I suppose you just cast up that bill in the fust place right off your uncle's books as they stood, didn't you?"

"Undoubtedly my sister did; for uncle's books were all kept in order," returned Hester, adding, "a great many visits charged there we did not bring into account, however, because uncle Jack had marked them with a star, signifying he meant to make a large deduction from the regular rates. They were usually visits to his poorer patients; and we have let them go, for the most part."

Dorothy would not have told this to whom it did not concern.

"Our account, your uncle's and mine, has run and run,— oh! run fer years." Mrs. Ruggles's tone implied that she would gladly have had it resemble the poet's brook, and "run on forever." She paused before she added persuasively, "There wasn't no stars scattered along in the course of mine, or was they some few?"

There were two in Hester's eyes as she answered, "There were *none*."

"Mebby not; but all the same this is a bill of *your* make, and not of hisen. When your uncle did fetch one in, he always used to let off on about one-quarter of it all told. He knowed how I was situate, — left a widdy-woman, with a great lot o' boys to bring up, and a big farm to see to besides. He considered it every time, dear old gentleman!"

"I like that system myself," said Hester in the

perfectly polite tones that Jack used to say meant "feathers and war-paint;" "only it does not go far enough. I would willingly drop charges for perhaps twenty or thirty visits my uncle made, — visits that meant wear and tear of himself and of his horse-flesh, cost of drugs and carriage-care, — if, when I went to the grocery to pay my bill, I could say, after the same fashion, "This bill has run so long, can't you cut off charges for about eight dozen eggs, and fifty pounds of butter, and all that cheese and soap and starch we have used up long ago?" and Hester looked placidly out of the window, across the "widdy-woman's" broad and fertile acres, thinking, "I am insisting, Dorothy, this time."

"Of course," replied Mrs. Ruggles. "Everybody wants their doo, and it is all right, only it is dreffle tight times. You — wouldn't be willing to turn that there note, would you? You see the crops sort of gin out last year, and ready money is so scass! But mebbe, now, if we could — kinder — turn it, you'd do just as well by yourselves as t'other way, and accommodate me a great deal better."

"How could we?" asked Hester, as prompt in tone as she was vague in comprehension.

The widow pushed her glasses off her light-green eyes, and betook herself to cogitation.

"You would not want some brown leghorns, for one thing, would you?"

Hester, with confused thoughts of straw bonnets, said, "No."

"Well, you just come with me a minute, and let me show you something," Mrs. Ruggles exclaimed enthusiastically. "I guess we can agree on it as sleek as a pin."

She seized a sun-bonnet off a peg behind the door, and signified to Hester that she should follow her down the back-steps, through the barnyard, where a flock of young turkeys joined them; and about twenty hens also, mistaking the widow's errand, ran cackling after. Behind a red barn, past three big haystacks, they came to a pasture, where she stopped, and leaned on the bars of the rail-fence. A little creek ran through the field; flat mossy stones edged its banks; a few low-boughed trees hung over it; and under them, luxuriating in the coolness, were five or six cows. Some were ankle-deep in the brown water, chewing the cud in content: others were clipping the crisp grass, their red sides glowing in the sunshine.

"Isn't that one a beauty?" said Mrs. Ruggles, pointing to a near cow. "She is the neatest-shaped creature you ever see, and playful as a kitten, unless you are a-milking of her: then she is as gentle as you please. You never set eyes on such milk as it is, — clear cream, it is so rich. And she gives a patent milk-pail brimming full twice a day. Did you ever hear the beat of *that?*"

"How much does a patent milk-pail hold?" asked Hester sagely.

"Hold? Why, about as much as you could stagger under. Now, that creature is a splendid breed, and I never should sell her if we did not want not to keep so many on 'em. S'pose, now, you take her, Miss Prescott? A body would think a family like your'n would take lots o' milk to cook with and to drink. Then there is cream fer berries, and butter if you ever make it. There ain't nothing like plenty of milk to save butchers' bills, if that's any account to you: 'tis to most folks."

Hester was strongly tempted. Perhaps the novelty of buying a cow, when she had hitherto only "shopped" for ribbons and pictures, moved her in some degree; then Granty was fond of *Charlotte russe*. But maybe it was not a good cow. Perhaps to buy a cow intelligently was to go all over it with a tape-measure, to look at its horns and hoofs, to count its teeth, and to put scientific questions in regard to all its points,—such questions as she had seen in "The American Agriculturist." Reflecting thus, she gave Mrs. Ruggles to understand, with equal modesty and truthfulness, that she was a mere amateur in cow-purchasing, and that, while to this cow in particular she felt somewhat inclined, she could not decide hastily.

"I tell you what," said Mrs. Ruggles: "just lemme call Myron. He's a professor. He won't tell you no fibs; but he will tell you all about them creaters, and which is the best on 'em. — *Myron, Myron!*"

Out from a near barn came a lank young person, who looked like his mother, and, like her, was clever, even if a little "near."

"Which is the best on 'em?" he repeated. "There ain't no best among 'em. Finest lot o' cows in the county. Most on 'em give twenty quarts a day. There ain't no calculatin' the butter we've made. Mother's broke down taking care of it, and that's the only reason we want to sell one or two on 'em off."

"Is this an imported cow?" asked Hester, that being the only question she could think of that sounded at all in keeping with the occasion.

"Wall — no — not exactly; but her ancestors must have been."

"Which cow do you mean, Mr. Ruggles?"

"Oh! any one on 'em: they are all number-one creaters. That ar red-legged one, now — she is worth sixty dollars. I tell you what, when you taste *that* cow's milk, every mouthful says it's cow's milk!"

"Oh! that is just what I do not want," cried Hester instantly. "If there is any thing that is disagreeable to me, it is milk that tastes cowy."

"My patience! Why, that's just the mark of a genewine cow. But women-folks is awful queer about such things. Wall, that speckly one by the old stump across there — she is mighty nigh a Flanders."

"Is she what is called a Flanders?" asked Hester briskly.

"Mighty nigh," reiterated the conscientious young man. "And that one over yonder, near her — she is to all intents an Ayrshire cow. Don't you see how fine her nose is between the muzzle and the eyes? Her legs are short, and her bones are fine; her joints are firm, and her shoulders are thin at the top; then her brisket is light, and her milk-veins are well defined. She is a prime one!"

"Does all that make her an Ayrshire cow?" asked Hester, resolved not to be swept away, but still somewhat stirred, by this sudden eloquence.

"Yes: them is all Ayrshire traits that I've been telling you, — them and some others."

"That may be, Mr. Ruggles. But did not this cow and all her ancestors originate on this or some other farm near here?"

Mr. Ruggles was honest, if he was trading cows. He came up to the question thus, —

"S'posen they did, Miss Prescott. If you was to

find a Jew up in the north pole, and all his relation there in the family buryin'-ground, wouldn't you allow he *was* a Jew, and not a Esquimau? It is the same way with Ayrshire cows, *exactly*."

Before Hester could rally, mother Ruggles interposed: "It is the little Jersey, Myron, that I know she'd set an awful store by if once she got it home, and tried the rich yaller milk. Look at her pretty head, and loving sort of eyes. — S'pose, Miss Prescott, you take this ere cow home to-day, and try her for a week. That lot behind your barn is good enough for a pasture; and, if you ain't just crazy to keep her, we'll take her back when you say the word, and pay the note cash down. If she does well, and you will have her, we'll call it square, and tear up the paper. Now, won't you let Myron show that boy out there with your horse how to lead her home, this very day, alongside o' you as you drive?"

Hester's face betrayed her desire to try the experiment; whereupon Myron chimed in, "Yes, Miss Prescott, she is as easily led as a lamb would be. Will you let me hitch a rope to her horns, and give it to the little boy?"

Hester said "*Yes;*" then, amazed at her own act, called to black Pete in a very calm way, "Come here, and see if you can do something."

Pete came, grinning with anticipation, and took

firm hold on the rope that Myron had brought from the barn, and tied to the cow. The pretty creature gazed mildly at him, and, with a stout pull, he started for the gate. Her part of the programme was, of course, to follow him; but, from some quick sense of insult, she made an agile revolution, and Pete very nearly stood upon his woolly head.

"Oh, pshaw now!" exclaimed Mrs. Ruggles. "Well, mebbe she *is* a little taken by surprise. — Myron, you better lead her down to the bend in the road, and she'll understand matters then, most likely."

Myron complied at once, and they started all together. It was Hester's intention to let Pete sit in the phaeton, after a while, and hold the rope-end, letting the cow amble along behind Old Mortality, whose gait could not be too rapid even for her. But it is always the "unexpected that happens." When Myron gave the rope into Pete's hands, all went well, and continued so for some time. Hester was just about to stop Old Mortality, and take Pete into the carriage, when the little African abruptly began a series of wild gymnastics that would have made an acrobat expire with envy. It is not supposable, that, if Pete should live a century, he could again, under any other circumstances, go so rapidly through so many revolutions, gyrations, circumambulations, and altogether aimless genuflections, as he carried on for the next five minutes. There was no mistaking the motive power. There was enough of what the French call *élan* in that meek-eyed little Jersey cow to have made a regiment resistless. All that Hester could do was to drive Old Mortality up to his knees in mayweed, and leave the road clear, that her companions might describe circles that resembled infinity, their centres being everywhere, and their circumferences nowhere. She cried out, full of fear, "Can you stand it, Pete? Oh, do, if you can!" About the time that he could not, the little cow calmed herself and went on, as if she were meek indeed. This happy condition of mind and body lasted for half a mile. Mortality stalked majestically on. Hester drove, with her head turned away from his solemnly vibrating tail, watching Pete in the rear, — Pete, whose wool was white with wayside dust, and whose eyes, like Iser's flood, were "rolling rapidly."

It happened, that, where they went, the farmhouses were few and far apart, and unfenced fields were all along the quiet road. Once Hester was betrayed into admiration of the beautiful swaying wheat, and forgot her fellow-travellers for the time being. Then a shadow — two of them — fled past her. There was a whir, a rattle, a sound of rushing feet, then silence, and only a flying cloud of dust left behind in the road.

"We've done gone into the wheat," came back faintly, in a minute.

"Have you let the rope go?" again called Hester.

"No: reckon I kin go whar she kin. We're a-restin'." And then she heard him add, in his retreat, "Call yerself a *cow*, do ye? Yer the swelled-up, cussinest old June bug ever flopped!"

"Yes, do rest," said Hester sympathetically. "It is hard on you, Pete, and I suppose you have crushed down just so much wheat anyway. That can't be helped."

They reposed so long, however, that she called at last, "Come, try again, Pete! If you get her safely home, you shall go to every circus this summer."

The cow was led forth, not unwillingly, and stepped along at an even rate for another mile, before she shot off into a marsh behind a thicket, from whence came the wail: "It's all *squashy*, an' I've los' my ole shoes: oooh!"

When they emerged, it was a long way ahead of the phaeton. The cow was bellowing wildly, and so was Pete: his spirit seemed to be broken.

"Can't you tie her to something?" cried Hester. "Do tie her to something, Pete, or she will kill you."

"She has!" howled Pete; and Hester, in the excitement, believed him. But there was just then a temporary calm: the cow entangled her own rope in a rail-fence, and had to come to a stand-still. Hester drove up to the spot, soothed Pete, sent him back after his shoes, and debated what they should do when he returned. To send Peter home alone to tell the tale, with African exaggerations, would be to have the entire family come out thinking to find her tossed, gored, and left dying by the wayside.

"Pete," she exclaimed, "you stay here, and watch the cow, while I drive home, and send a man back for it."

"No!" roared Pete instantly. "I'm scared of her all 'lone. 'Pears like the debble mought be in her. Mammy's seen debbles git inter cattle heaps o' times. I'd radder run her longside o' compny."

"Well, then, if you can stand it, we will. You shall have a whole pie when we get home, sweetened with molasses, as you like it best."

Thus sustained and soothed, Pete said that he could go on immediately; but what a going that was, taken as a whole! To be sure, the Jersey cow had lucid intervals, when she paced along by sober Old Mortality, and they seemed to be two beasts with but a kindred thought. But again she whirled poor Pete down an embankment, and through a stony ravine; she whisked him over an acre of Canada thistles, and broke down a rail-fence by a judicious application of him as a battering-ram: but we are so glad to say they reached home about three o'clock in the afternoon. The cow and Peter came first. She plunged through the front-gate, upset an urn of flowers, and, finding herself really free, stopped under the veranda where Granty sat reading Jeremy Taylor's "Holy Living." Pete flung himself on the grass, and, to her perplexity and her questions, responded only by groaning, and waving his hand in the direction of the North Road, down which, like a very high-toned funeral, Old Mortality was decorously proceeding.

"What does this mean, Hester?" said the old lady. "Why don't Pete drive this creature out?"

"It is the way the widow Ruggles turned her note," was the enigmatical answer; and, for more information, Granty followed to the kitchen, where Hester told Bridget O'Flarity first of her exploits, and Bridget rubbed her big red hands in glee.

"Arrah, now!" she would like to see the cow that would not love her. "In course the crayture couldn't take kindly to a hathen with the face of Pete." She would make her "swate-mannered as a dove," once she "had a hand on her:" so out she went to entice her into the barn to coax and pet her into docility. Granty was busy enough with Pete. He was told he need not move again that day. He was offered liniment and arnica and hamamelis. He was encouraged to refresh himself at once with beefsteak, strawberry short-cake, and pork and beans, with side-dishes many and varied. As soon as the arrival was published throughout the house, the family followed Miss O'Flarity to the barn.

Dorothy gazed at the animal doubtfully. Granty and Marion were inclined to think Hester had been wise in bringing her home. Jack, like a large and troublesome fly, was under and over and all about her, finally shrieking, "Let us call her Buttercup, dear little Buttercup;" and they did then and there.

We need only add, that, when her first natural excitement died out, she proved to be in all respects the kind of cow that the widow Ruggles had declared her to be; and, after a week of trial, they decided to keep her for their own.

CHAPTER V.

Which introduces a New-England Person.

"HESTER, do you like ministers?" asked Granty one morning.

"Oh, yes! Are they not just as good as other Christians when they behave themselves?"

"Of course, child. What a singular speech!"

Jack looked up from a boat he was whittling to see if she meant him; then he remarked, "Granty had a minister here to see her yesterday; not ours, either."

"Did you? Who was he," asked Hester.

"Mr. Severn, the new pastor of the Old First Church. His family are Massachusetts people; and he knows, as I found out, very many members of old families in Boston and Cambridge, with whom I am connected over and over again by marriages. We had a delightful conversation." And Granty sat even more erect as she added, "I have not met a person with whom I was so well pleased in a long time."

Hester was secretly wondering what the *old* gentleman could have wanted. She did not think he might be young. So in a moment she said, "He has been in town only a few weeks. Is it not queer for him to call so soon on strangers who are not in his church?"

"I do not think it is strange at all. Did not every minister come sooner or later to see your uncle? Even the priest and the rabbi used to call."

"He was everybody's friend; and *we* are women."

"There was reason enough this gentleman should call on *me*, and I hope to see more of him hereafter," she added significantly.

Marion mischievously asked, "Why did you not call us into the room to see the old gentleman?"

"*Old?* He is not more than thirty-five or forty. You will have chances enough to see him. We talked so fast I forgot you."

"If he does not preach to us, we shall not be very likely to see him," said Hester.

Granty now struggled between her desire to say something and her fear that it would not be well received. Jack helped her out of the difficulty in a way peculiar to himself.

"I think," he observed off-hand, "that he is a mighty queer fellow. He came along — I was a-settin' on the horse-block "—

"Sitting" (Marion).

"Sottin'" (Jack). "Well, sitting on the block;

and he began to ask, 'Does Mrs. — Mrs. — Mrs.' — (then he could not tell for the life of him who) 'live in here?' I said, 'Prescott?' He asked if she was a *widow*. I said there was four of them inside there."

"Why, Jack! There is not a widow here but Granty."

"Well, what *are* you, then? There isn't any husband to any of you. Would you have had me said you were all old maids? I can't tell what you are, I'm sure!"

"Are we not all young and beautiful, and in our prime?" cried Marion with comic sternness.

"I didn't know you were so awful young. You all of you are nice enough; but you might be widows, couldn't you?"

"Certainly. But go on with your story."

"Wall, he said he was looking for an elderly widow who lived along here. I said Granty was about ninety; then I said no, she couldn't be, because she sees and hears and eats, and don't walk on a wooden leg, as old Mrs. Weeks does. I said I presumed she was about forty or fifty."

"Jack!" expostulated Granty, her eyes very brilliant, "to say I went on a wooden leg!"

"No: I explained that you *didn't*. Next thing he asked if there was anybody here except your own family. You see, he did not know I lived here. I said yes; that you had one old red horse, called Mortality, that, on a steady go, could beat any trotting caterpillar he ever heard of; and a litle nig" —

"Jack Prescott!"

"And a little colored boy that Old Mortality made faces at, and a girl from the north of Ireland, because Granty liked those best. Then I remembered him — you know, down in the closet: so I said there was a pretty old skeleton that lacked a few ribs, so he was not all there; but the most of him had been in the family thirty years, though he really did not belong to it in the first place. I was going to tell him about Hester's cow; but he got to laughing awfully: so I walked off, and left him to find out the rest for himself."

The girls were divided between mirth at Jack and surprise at Mr. Severn's questions.

"What curiosity he must have!" said Hester. "I am glad Granty did not call us into the room."

"Now, the sum and substance of it all is just this," confessed Granty. "He was looking for a boarding-place, and some one told him that we might take him. I, of course, assured him that we had never done such a thing in all our lives as to take an outsider into the family. He made a very polite apology for asking; said he never would have ventured to call, had he not supposed the person who sent him had good reasons for so doing."

"A boarder!" exclaimed Marion, "and a minister at that. Think of it!"

"Yes. I told him you girls would think about it."

"Oh! how could you, Granty?" cried Hester.

"Because I did not know that it would do to say 'yes' right on the spot. To be sure, a person would think I might take that much responsibility; but I frequently find we do not all think alike."

"It never occurred to me that you wanted to keep a boarding-house," said Hester naughtily.

Granty's indignation was extreme. "*I* keep a boarding-house? I should think you were beside yourself! It is a very different thing to take in a clergyman as a favor, when the poor man does not wish to be running around among strangers seeking a home. His father knew old Judge Wentworth, and he was often invited there when he was a child. He distinctly remembered members of the Leggett family I have so often spoken of. I do not know how you look upon the matter; but *I* think that for a parcel of women to live in these days with no man about the house is pretty unsafe. It was only last night I heard queer noises in the back-cellar near the vinegar-barrel; and I have my suspicions that a jar of pickled peaches has been removed."

"Nevertheless," said wicked Hester, "it seems to me that it would do just as well to keep a rat-terrier for such cases as a minister."

"I have nothing further to say on the subject. Do exactly as you see fit," said Granty with severe dignity. "Jack, bring me the last-evening paper."

"Do you think, Granty," asked Marion in her most conciliating way, "that Mr. Severn felt encouraged by any thing said?"

"I neither told him that he could, nor that he could not. Do not let us have any more words on the subject."

"How lovely these roses are over the piazza!" remarked Marion, after a pause. Parting the lace curtains, she stepped out of the window, and sat down in a rustic chair, whither she knew Dorothy or Hester would probably soon follow. They did; and Hester began immediately, "How do you suppose she left the question? Perhaps the next thing will be the arrival of a barrel of sermons, a theological library, and a dyspeptic clergyman. I could not endure it; could you?"

"Of course not. But what shall we do? We cannot send him word not to come if he has no idea of coming."

"Suppose," said Dorothy reflectively, "that we let him come. He might be agreeable, and no trouble. Granty would enjoy his society; and his board-bill would come in very well."

"Never!" said Hester. "Marion's old German

teacher used to say she was a 'unique.' I think we are a family of 'uniques' in some respects; but I am not a bit proud of it. I only realize forcibly that any clerical person with clear-starched manners and well-regulated mind would be rendered unfit for his duties by abiding with us; or else we would — But nonsense, Dorothy, you know we won't have him anyway! We are all peculiarly adapted to be by ourselves, I think. There is Granty — we love and respect her: but we often laugh about her; we can't help it. All the time we know she is very intelligent, a perfect lady, and a 'steadfast old Christian,' as Lamb says. But do you suppose that we would let anybody outside the family, who did not appreciate her, find her amusing? He couldn't help it. He would expire if he did not laugh sometimes; and, if he did, I would annihilate him." And, ending, Hester looked as belligerent as if a general assembly of divines were engaged in ridiculing them as a family.

The gate shut with a slam: a gentleman walked leisurely under the trees toward the open front-door. The girls glanced through the screen of rosebushes; and Dorothy whispered, "It is Mr. Severn. — You go, Marion: my dress is all tumbled after my strawberry-picking."

"No, I do not want to see him: let Hester."

Hester was willing. But Dorothy was reluctant to

have her go and despatch the poor man, if Granty had encouraged him. Upon certain occasions, and usually with strangers, Hester had about the affability of the sphinx; and, unless they were her inferiors, she would be the grimmest, stiffest, and most noncommittal of mortals. Dorothy was the reverse of all this in manner. You felt sure, after being introduced to her, that she must have heard of you before, and that favorably: later you were sure she was a person whose good opinion flattered you. There was scarcely a widower, young or old, who was "looking around," that ever by chance encountered Dorothy, who did not soon ask after her, call at the office on uncle Jack, or boldly try his fortunes with her, always hitherto without success.

To-day, seeing Hester glance at the front-door with a look that said, "'Twere well it were done quickly," and half arise, Dorothy resolved to forget her slightly tumbled dress, and instantly glided past her sisters, across the parlor, and into the wide old hall. She met Mr. Severn at the door with a genial smile, and gave him the great easy-chair that always stood ready for chance-comers. He was a tall man, with a strong, rugged face, clear, pleasing eyes, and a good mouth, with character enough in his features to make him seem older than he could have been. He wore no gloves, but carried them, and was not the kind of man who suggested cloth, ministerial or otherwise.

"Perhaps, Miss Prescott," he said simply, "I owe you the same apology I made your mother yesterday. I do not like my noisy rooms at the hotel, and I was told that I might make some arrangement for quieter ones here. I felt as if I had taken a great liberty yesterday when I found that you had never had any one as a boarder; but your mother was kind enough to say she would think of the matter, and I might call again."

"Yes, sir. Aunt Prescott told us of your call, and how much she enjoyed it. She usually finds a friend in one who comes from Massachusetts. Well, it is just this, Mr. Severn, aunt Prescott is well, but not very strong; and she takes, at any rate, so much care upon herself, that we think it best to keep the house rather quiet, and prevent her from overtaxing herself; and — and to do this — we — we " —

Not having rehearsed her part, Dorothy was taken at a disadvantage, and was coming out, she knew not where. The color rushed into her cheeks, and she gasped, but only for a second. Sedately, and as a matter of course, Mr. Severn broke in, —

"Yes: you mean that you like being quite by yourselves. I should think it would make the housekeeping easier: an outsider always does make a difference. Your aunt and I will be friends hereafter, Miss Prescott; for we did have a very delightful chat. She carried me back to times and people I like to remember; and she lent me a book I have not seen since I read it in my father's garret, — one day when I was shut up there for some misdemeanor. It is a copy of the 'New-England Memorial,' and with it a curious account of King Philip's war. I sat up very late last night re-reading it, and do not know when a quaint book has interested me more."

Dorothy said she had read it a long while before, and as briskly as possibly continued a conversation that should detain him long enough to leave a pleasant impression. His quick instincts had served him so well, he had saved her the need of saying in so many words, "You cannot board here;" and she was very grateful to him. When he went away, he said, "Please tell your aunt I have papers often sent me from the towns we talked of, and I shall bring her the next I receive."

He lingered, like a friend, a moment at the door, plucked a rose, and, meeting Jack on his way to the gate, greeted him with sincere warmth, and a peculiar smile that Dorothy understood better than if Jack had not reported their previous interview.

"Well," asked Marion, "what is he like, Dorothy?"

"He is the kind of a man uncle Jack would say had no nonsense about him. I liked him."

"Were you sorry to send him away?"

"Oh, no! Only he would not have been a dreadful creature in the house."

"Perhaps not," spoke Hester, from the pages of a new art journal. "But what do we want of a man?"

"I want him to get out on the roof," answered Granty, appearing suddenly in the door,—"to get out and tie a scraper of some sort to a rope, and drag it up and down the chimney to dislodge the soot. When the wind blows, it falls down into the parlor grate, and looks just like preserved plums,—for what reason I am sure I cannot say."

"You dear old lady!" cried Hester, "you shall have a man up there. If you will keep him on the roof, he may stay there forever."

"How ridiculous you are, Hester! It will not take a man ten minutes, and I hope you will see to it immediately."

Hester promised she would.

CHAPTER VI.

Granty takes her " Turn."

"HESTER," said Marion, appearing in the studio one day, "I want an idea, and you must suggest it to me. My story has gone so far, and suddenly the interest fails. I am outside of my people, pulling them about like puppets: I must have a new impulse. Listen!"

Seating herself on a chair, from which Hester rescued, just in time, a bottle of turpentine, Marion began,—saying, "This is about in the middle: I read you some of the first once,—' Lucian chose Ethel's favorite books, and read them to her as if he had written them himself. In music, with his exquisite'"—

"Who were Lucian," put in Hester, "and Ethel? I don't remember them."

"Oh! I believe I did call them John and Susan in the first chapter: I cannot be all the time looking back after their names, until I revise and copy," returned Marion, going rapidly on with a few more pages of her manuscript.

"Lucian, or Adolphus, or what you may call him, is a stick," said Hester coolly. "There is no more blood in him than there is in a gilded liberty-pole. Did you ever see anybody in the least like him?"

"No. But I undertook to create a character, Hester."

"Humph! Well, I like your men who *are* like other men. Stop, and let me show you a similar effort of my own. Study it, and tell me what it is." So saying, Hester searched among her treasures, and brought forth a moderately large canvas, which she held up before her sister. Marion, after a grave examination, said, "It is a pterodactyl. My geology says its anterior foot is the expansor of a membranous wing."

Hester laughingly replaced the picture, saying, "That is the one effort of *my* creative genius. I felt sure that I could portray Shelley's Queen Mab, 'moving on the moving air,' ethereal, exquisite, diaphanous, (isn't that the word?) and all that, you know. Yes, it is very much like a pterodactyl. I was humbled by that, and taught to know my limitations. It is better for me in art to make faithful studies of mud-turtles that I have seen than to undertake flying fairies I have not seen. Perhaps it may be so in literature with you."

"Verily, now, I think you may be right," said Marion. "I am bored by my hero; and I believe I will tear him up, and make another, after the fashion of common men. But what are you painting now, Hester?"

Hester stepped back from her work to let Marion come nearer, and, in her turn, express decided disapprobation. On the easel were two photographs,— one of a good-natured, big-eyed man, with light hair elaborately brushed, with awkward large hands crossed on his breast, and a general air of rusticity and good clothes. The other picture, evidently thrown up from an old daguerrotype, was of a moon-faced woman. It was whity blank where shadows should be, void of expression, and grotesque with the fashion of a dress long out of date.

"What do you paint such caricatures for, Hester?"

"Did not Dorothy tell you what I was doing? I was reading in the piazza one day last week, when a man (the original of this photograph) opened the gate, came up the walk, and asked if the young woman that worked in oil was 'to home.' I knew what he wanted, when he said that he was Mr. Jerry Scudder, and that Uncle Jack once told him that I could paint photographs. Here 'was his, and there was *hers*. His was taken the week before: hers was from a picture taken fifteen years before.' She was dead, and he wished her photograph painted as a companion-piece to his own. He explained it all, with a faith in me that was quite touching. He said, 'I'd like to have you fix her to look as she would, if she have lived up to date.'

"I said I could not; but he declared that I could. He said I must paint off those 'long, loose ringlets that ain't worn now, and put on frizzles along the seam of her head, you know.' Couldn't I do that? I said perhaps I could, if that was all. No: her family all had weak eyes when they 'got along about so far,' and wore gold glasses. Now, Elizabeth would look more natural and 'nowadays-like' to him in eye-glasses, could that be managed. It appeared to me a great liberty to take with the late Mrs. Scudder, — 'she as was a Perry,' so he said, — but, if her husband insisted, I could not refuse. The longer he talked, the droller it seemed, and I became actually interested in the task he set for me. The unpainted old dress is hideous; but, after I have done my best with her face, I shall put on a neat black dress and lace collar, instead of that plaid with huge frills."

"Yes. And at last who will she be, I would like to know?" asked Marion.

"Oh! it will not be a *be*, but a *might have been*," said Hester absurdly. "And you need not 'tip tilt' your nose at it, either; for I view these in a practical way. I am to have ten dollars each for them. Mr. Scudder's ruffled shirt-front and seal-ring represent roasts, puddings, possibly potatoes "—

"O Hester, don't! you make me sick," protested Marion.

At that moment the door opened quickly, and Dorothy looked in, asking, " Have either of you been down stairs this morning?"

"No," replied Hester, "not since breakfast. I have been painting, and Marion has been busy too, — with her writing."

"And I," said Dorothy regretfully, — "I went down town, and staid longer than I intended. I have just come home, and was talking to Granty, when I saw that little tin box in which we keep our important papers, in the dining-room on the table. I asked why it was there, and she said that old Mrs. Kempshall from Sandy Hill came in to pay her note."

"Did she?" asked Hester, interested at once. "But how could Granty attend to it without sending for us? She is not an executor, you know."

"Do you think that would make any difference with her? What Granty desires to execute she executes, as you ought to know by this time."

"Well, never mind," said Marion, "if the woman only paid the twenty dollars."

Dorothy seemed to struggle with varied emotions; then she left them as abruptly as she had come, only saying, "Girls, she *turned* it; but it is not a cow."

Marion looked wonderingly at Hester, saying, "What can it be, do you think?"

"A panorama of the Holy Land; a dromedary, it may be. Let us go and find out," was Hester's reply.

They descended to the room, where Granty sat reading Bogatzky's "Golden Treasury."

"You see, girls," she began at once, "my aunt Leggett used to have one quite similar in some respects. They are regarded as rather a nice thing to have in a family. I have often heard aunt Leggett tell of hers. It was the time Lafayette was in this country; and he staid over night in her house, and slept under just " —

"Beg your pardon, Granty; but has old Mrs. Kempshall been here this morning?" asked Marion.

"Yes, she has, to see about that note we held against her. She is a good old soul, and I would not grind the face of the poor for all the world."

"Certainly not. However, Mrs. Kempshall is not poor, should anybody want to inflict that injustice upon her countenance," said Hester.

"Well, she told me what dreadful work she had

with her crops last year. She could not get men enough to help her, either, and she had to run a — a some sort of a fan herself, hands were so scarce."

Dorothy, in a cold-blooded way, said that rich farmers always had bad work with their crops; and Hester bewildered the poor old lady by saying that nobody but heathen nabobs had their fanning done for them.

"She suggested, did she not," added Marion, "that uncle Jack always cut down her bills, and" —

"She did," returned Granty briskly. "And then she went on, you know, and said, if I would only consider that this represented several years' work; and the separate pieces — Well, really, it was curious to hear their history. They came from about every family in the country: often they were little odds and ends a dressmaker would give her."

"The *country — dressmaker*," Hester was echoing doubtfully.

Dorothy reached after something behind her, then, as if waving a banner, spread out on the carpet one of the most singularly ugly bedquilts that ever the brain of a woman devised. It was formed of uneven stars, of every shade imaginable, of silk, satin, velvet, wool, even cotton, when "odds and ends" ran low, or the dressmaker was not abroad. These stars were recklessly besprinkled over a butternut-brown firmament, bounded, however, as the upper firmament is not, and that by a pink gimp frayed enough to hint of some service in the past.

Hester and Marion viewed it with amazement, mute at first. The edge of Dorothy's emotion had been already somewhat blunted: so she said nothing. At last Marion found breath to ask, "At what did Mrs. Kempshall value this work of art?"

"Why, she said," continued Granty, "that it was not just the cost of each little piece; but taking the choice of colors and the commingling of them, — oh, yes! and the *associations*, she spoke of them" —

"Did she leave them too?" said Hester sternly. "I will not have them — not one! Nobody shall pass their old associations over to me, no matter what they may attempt with their old bedspreads. I can form new ones for myself."

"Why, you never made a bedspread in your life, Hester!"

"Granty, I was only talking of associations. Please go on with old Mrs. Kempshall."

"She set it all before me, — her troubles of one sort and another. She is land-poor, whatever that is; and the upshot of it all was, she proposed to turn this on the bill, and call it square. What else could we do? It is elaborate, as you can see for yourselves; and, if she thought it was beautiful, you would not wish me to have hurt the poor creature's feelings by sneering at it."

"Did you give up the note, Granty?" asked Hester.

"I did, and she destroyed it before my eyes."

"What for, Granty?"

"Why, to show me, I suppose, that she would never give us any more trouble," returned the old lady, with an expression of worldly shrewdness that was irresistible. "Now really, girls, you need not scoff at that quilt," she protested to the young women, whose feelings were finding expression in peals of laughter. "I have seen homelier ones in my day, many a one worse by far."

"Do you want it on your bed?" asked Marion, deceitfully generous.

"No—o. I have become so used to white Marseilles, I cannot say that I do; but as a very curious thing, you know— Either of you can take it," she added with equally prompt generosity.

When the three had refused it with ungrateful unanimity, the old lady placidly remarked, "Well, if none of you like it, I will tell you what we can do. Stuffed with cotton, it could be made into a warm 'comfortable,' and you can put it into the next Home Missionary box that goes West."

Dorothy made her tones very bland indeed before

she suggested: "It is done now, so it is of no great consequence; but after this, Granty, it will save you trouble, when people come on business, to call one of us. I suppose, according to form of law, only one of the executors can settle uncle Jack's bills."

"Oh, fiddlesticks!" quoth Granty. "Do you suppose I can't attend to my own brother's affairs, without asking what the law allows? I think I shall do that much while I have my right mind, executor or not." Then she looked for her glasses that she had put in her pocket, and went to see herself if Bridget properly flavored the custard for dinner.

"I call *that* an outrageous swindle," said Marion, when the door shut behind her. "The old schemer saw how innocent-minded Granty was, and just victimized us all. Probably she only hoped to get this starry monstrosity in for some small part of the amount."

"I have a mind," said Dorothy, "to take it straight back to her, and make her ashamed of herself."

"No," said Hester slowly. "Let the stingy soul go: uncle Jack would, I presume. Don't you remember the man who insisted on paying his bill in pop-corn, bags and bags of it, and he let him do it?"

She mused a while, then suddenly exclaimed, "I have a 'home mission' for the thing. Come and see, girls!"

She picked the spread from the carpet, and bore it away, followed by Dorothy, as far as the office. Upon arriving there, Hester opened the door, behind which dangled the poor old "bone man," as Jack often called him. Hanging one end of the gay drapery to a peg above his head, she let the soft folds completely envelope the rattling remains of him, and explained to Dorothy, "There! isn't that well? It occurred to me the other day, that people not expecting such an apparition might be startled if they came suddenly on the family ghost. Now a glance in here will not scare the most sensitive; and if anybody has the impudence to be prying around, without leave or license, they deserve to see all they can. Poor old fellow, you are welcome to your covering." And Hester turned away, feeling that in some way she was "even" with Mrs. Kempshall.

"After all," she added, "the ugliness of the bedspread does not impress me half so much as the 'associations' she threw in. The idea of shuffling them off on strange parties is — is simply delicious in its audacity."

The dinner-bell summoned them at this point, and they went back to tell Granty what had been done. She was as much gratified as if she had taken the thing with direct reference to this end. She wondered that she had not reflected before this, that it was very shocking to have the skeleton exposed to chance callers.

Marion reconstructed her story in the afternoon; but more than once she laid down her pen to laugh outright at the last "turn" Granty had given to their affairs. How uncle Jack would have roared over such an occurrence!

It was this same afternoon, however, that Jack brought from the post-office a letter for Marion, containing a check for twenty-five dollars: so all was well. Moreover, the editor of "The Flying Courier" was "pleased to have received another story from" her "graceful pen, and would" she "favor" them "occasionally in the future?"

She would, inasmuch as her graceful pen had undertaken to scatter just such favors far and wide.

CHAPTER VII.

Aunt Pepperfield's Nieces.

"NOT one of us has written to aunt Huldah in a long time," said Hester one day; "and she likes to be kept informed of every thing that happens to us."

"It is such a task for me to write letters!" said Dorothy. "I think Marion ought to do it: her hand is in all the time."

"And for that very reason, when I am tired of copy, I am not free for correspondence," answered Marion. Nevertheless, that same afternoon she wrote to aunt Huldah Pepperfield.

She had gone to her room for another purpose, and was sitting with her desk, so that the breeze that fanned the white curtain could reach her, and whenever she raised her eyes she might catch a glimpse of the outer world, a quiet bit of it, only made up of the long village street, where the trees met overhead, where the grass grew each side of the road, and little children played safely there; birds twittered, and dandelions blossomed, only now and then a carriage passed.

"What are you at now?" asked Hester, in passing her door.

"Oh! a short article, not a story this time, for Mr. Winthrop Craig."

"And who might Mr. Winthrop be?"

"He is, as I have only just found out, the editor, or one of them, of 'The Phœnix.' I like his own articles very much, and I am conceited enough to think that he might like mine. I shall give him a chance to find out whether he would or not, at any rate."

Marion wrote out in full his address on an envelope, and put it on a pile of manuscripts.

"I wish you could take time to write to aunt Pepperfield," said Hester, going on.

"I will do it now," called Marion after her.

She took a sheet of paper from that on which she had been writing her article, and began at once. An hour later she was surprised to hear the tea-bell ring; but she had accomplished her undertaking. Now, it was one of Miss Marion's habits to direct her envelopes before or during the process of writing her letters. She had done so this afternoon; but, forgetful of the fact that she had directed two for different persons, she reached out for one, took that addressed to the editor of "The Phœnix," hurried into it aunt Huldah Pepperfield's letter, thrust it into her pocket, and went gayly down stairs. An hour later in the twilight, she gave it to Jack, who straightway hied him to the post-office; and the next mail carried into an editor's sanctum a missive more singular than any one of the remarkable and ambiguous effusions continually arriving there for editorial examination. Of its reception we will tell later.

Aunt Huldah was Granty's sister, and in past years had been her equal in position and authority in this their brother's household; but, upon reaching the age of fifty, she responded to the affection of an excellent widower, and became Mrs. Pepperfield. The girls had been very sorry to part with her. There was as much repose in her nature as there was restlessness in Granty's. She always expected things to come out right, sang cheerful hymns in most ecstatic discords, and was always willing to let "the girls" do any thing they thought proper. Her home was now near New-York City; and her nieces frequently made her long visits.

In these days Hester finished the pictures of Mrs. and Mr. Jerry Scudder, to the great satisfaction of the latter. During the process of coloring he had called many times on as many comical errands; so that the young ladies became very well acquainted with him. Once he brought a sample of plaid poplin, a bit of his wife's dress, to copy; but Dorothy convinced him a dark, plain dress was preferable. Again, he did not know but his wife's relations might "object to the gold specs, as she never really did wear them: could they be taken off?" On another occasion he had been to a city photographer's, and had seen "folks all sort of enveloped in a cloud," and questioned whether he had better be done up in that style, or left with folded hands and velvet vest. He decided, after looking again at his seal-ring, not to be enveloped, but to have "her finished up so," because it seemed "more appropriate."

Hester's patience, her attention, and her answers, were all in very short metre; but Dorothy always kindly invited Mr. Scudder to sit down, and talk over each detail to his heart's content. He was a clever, honest-hearted man, with good sense when one struck it squarely. When the pictures were done, he paid for them promptly, and delicately enough even for Hester's pride. The next week he returned with seven more photographs: six were those of his interesting family of girls and boys taken singly; the seventh was a family-group of the whole, arranged like a row of assorted ninepins. All of these he earnestly entreated that Hester would "attend to while her paint and oil was running." He also brought

Dorothy an enormous bunch of early summer flowers, of which he talked appreciatively. Moreover, he told her, rather in an aside suggestive of confidence, that he remembered when she was a "little tow-headed thing, riding around in her uncle's gig, and, if she would allow him, he would say she had "*handsomed up* considerably" since then. She frankly admitted she was glad to know it; and she graciously thanked him for inviting Granty and her to ride out and see his "place" some day. Indeed, Granty and Dorothy were extremely social, and kept themselves more in contact with outsiders than did Hester and Marion. People thought Hester peculiar and a wee bit sarcastic; while Marion was to many only "the woman who wrote." They always expected to ask her if she had read this essay, or liked that author. They secretly wondered if she would not put them in a story; and they never failed to inquire if she was "busy with her pen," or to ask her "how many hours a day she wrote, and if it came easy for her."

One beautiful afternoon the ladies were all at home, and sitting together in the great cool hall that ran directly through the house. The front-door opened on to a broad piazza overlooking the lawn; and from the door at the opposite end of the hall one could step into an arbor of roses and honeysuckle. The floor of the hall itself was dark, polished wood; the chairs tall, Gothic, and most substantial. A gay Chinese screen gave color to the place; and high up on the dark red wall hung a goodly array of ancestors (New-England persons every one). The ladies, as they sat sewing and reading in the summer air and fragrance, had no need to be ashamed of these voiceless relatives in ruffled shirts and gay brocades; while they, in turn, had they not had eyes that saw not, — they would have looked approvingly on Granty in her brisk, genteel old ladyhood; on Hester, whose eye had the gleam of the great-uncle over her head (whose surgeon's knife was said not to have been keener than his wit); or Dorothy, with the genial face of the grandmother renowned for her charming tea-parties; or Marion, who might have copied her straight nose and grave mouth from the pale minister painted in his study-cap, with finger in a theological tome. But speaking of ministers brings to mind that Granty had just been wondering where Mr. Severn found a boarding-place, when voices were heard coming near, and Marion murmured, "The Howell girls are coming!"

In a moment two young ladies appeared in the piazza, were greeted cordially, and made comfortable.

"I am very glad you have come in," said Granty. "I told Hester yesterday that we had not been in your house in a long time, and it was very unneighborly; but there is so much to do in the spring of the year, you know!"

"Yes, indeed! We have been very busy ourselves," said the youngest, — Miss Maude.

She was a yellow blonde, with an eye for effect. Her jewels were barbaric; bits of old gold-colored satin lighted up her black drapery; and she was studying "art" at this period of her interesting existence. Her elder sister, Miss Blanche, was large and white and serene: she intended to be. She considered it her life-work to take large, serene, and sweet (very sweet) views of almost every thing, beginning, of course, at herself. She, too, responded with gentle slowness to Granty's words, saying, —

"Yes, we have been negligent ourselves; but we have found *Mr. Severn* so interesting! *Such* an addition to our family, that we have really staid close at home to enjoy him."

"Mr. Who?" asked Granty quickly.

"Why, the new East-End minister," returned Maude, glad to note that the pale-blue panel of the Chinese screen was behind her golden hair. "The idea of our taking a boarder is too exquisitely ridiculous, I do admit; but the poor man could not find any sort of a home with congenial society. I am just perfectly fascinated by him. Yes, I am, Miss Dorothy! You need not laugh: you would be yourself;" and, with an arch toss of her head, Miss Maude turned now to Marion, and gayly confided this sentiment: "Men of heart, and at the same time of real culture, are not so common. I said to mother, 'Now we have found one, do let us befriend him.' You know how it is, Miss Marion. This town is full of real lovable persons (I would not breathe a word against them for the world); but for oh — ah — well, sympathetic companionship, one must look elsewhere. For instance, I have lately been all swallowed up in Byzantine art; but goodness me! who cared a straw about conversing with me? — Isn't it really disheartening, Miss Hester?"

"It might be, if I had to talk on Byzantine art."

"Oh, you naughty, sarcastic girl!" began Maude; but Granty interposed: "I like Mr. Severn very much. I would have taken him in here gladly; but it was not very convenient."

"We had plenty of room," remarked Blanche, "and it would have been selfish not to have admitted him, when we were entreated to by some of his friends. Mother dotes on clergymen herself; and then, as sister says, it is a pleasure to have such people with one socially. We asked him last evening to read to us, and he chose something out of a book of selections on the table, and he read it so finely! It was something about — oh — the transmigration of souls, I believe — very uncommon style."

Marion looked curious; and Maude said, "It was by Wordsworth, Blanche, was it not?"

"Oh! 'Intimations of immortality,' perhaps," said Marion, but not before Granty was softly chanting off on her knitting-needles, —

> "Our birth is but a sleep and a forgetting:
> The soul that rises with us, our life's star,
> Hath had elsewhere its setting,
> And cometh from afar."

One would do well who could find poetry of that kind that Granty could not repeat without a slip. Maude looked a little surprised, as she often did, when she discovered that what to her was new riches must have always been current coin in this family.

"I met Mr. Severn once," said Dorothy; "and he seemed to me a very kindly man, and a strong one intellectually."

"Oh, he is *deep!* He is just as deep as he can be," solemnly affirmed Maude. "We have not been able to speak of a thing he did not know about."

Hester looked so wicked, that Dorothy was glad Blanche added immediately, before she could speak, "Yes; and he is easy to get along with too; not at all preachy, or much of a talker, either. I told him all about *you* last night, Marion, — what you were like, and all that, you know. What are you engaged on now?"

"I am making the belt to a cambric morning-dress."

"Dearie me!" put in Maude. "She means your *literary* work. Now, how do you carry it on, tell us, please? Do you sit up half the night, drink strong coffee, get more and more wrought up, go to bed toward daylight, with your brains throbbing and wild visions careering" —

"Nothing careers in this house at night," laughed Marion, "unless it is Granty. She arises often to add some new dish to the bill of fare for breakfast. The rest of us go to bed at ten o'clock. I drink my coffee in the morning; I write by sunlight; and I never have throbs or visions, or any remarkable manifestations at all."

Maude surveyed the lady with abated interest. Evidently she had no genius, or she would have had an eccentricity or two.

Blanche, studying the blush rose in the bosom of her white dress, asserted with a tender smile, "I often think I will take up authorship; but I should fail in the drudgery of copying, and all that. My graduating composition was read by a gentleman who said I ought to send it to 'The Atlantic Monthly.' It was on 'The Heart's True Penetralia.' I don't think my gift would lie so much in story-writing as in essays like Macaulay's. It is a great field, a vast field!"

"Whose field?" said Granty suddenly. Having lost a few stitches off her needle, she had also lost the run of Blanche's remark.

"Literature, Granty, literature," said Dorothy, adding, "How is your sister Molly? She does not come to see us as often as she used to come when uncle Jack was alive."

"She has been busy sewing. Mother would prefer to have our work done out of the house; but Molly likes to sew better than to read. Who makes your dresses, Miss Marion?"

"I make them myself."

"You don't tell me so! *Why*, I never supposed you ever set a stitch, or did any thing but read or write."

Marion sighed with calm resignation. Almost three hundred and sixty-five times each year, for ten years, some acquaintance had made this speech to her. After refuting it three thousand six hundred and fifty times as a sort of personal insult, she succumbed; and now she let people go on supposing that a pen in a woman's hand acts as a complete paralyzer of her whole being; that she could not sew two fig-leaves together, if her costume depended on it; could not cook a mouthful of food, if she starved; could not give a dose of medicine, or wash a baby's face, or — be any thing, in short, but a penholder.

"Well," said Dorothy, "if you want to be enlightened, I can tell you, that, when Marion wants a new dress, she does not ask anybody's leave or license. She goes out and buys it with her own money; then she gets the latest fashion-book, and makes fun of it; next she studies some stylish friend's attire, — some one whose taste she approves (often yours or Blanche's); then she cuts boldly into her cloth, and comes out looking as well as anybody."

"Well, I am astonished!" exclaimed Maude; and then she gave her attention to Hester, of whom she was always a trifle afraid, but therefore desired all the more to study her nature and habits. In a little while, with the hesitant affability of one offering an elephant a tit-bit, she said tentatively, "And you, Miss Hester, — you find art *so* fascinating! You love it, don't you?"

"I don't know any thing about it," returned Hester grimly. Little affectations always made her as stiff as a grenadier.

"Why, I thought you painted, and read Ruskin and — and Mrs. Jameson, and" —

Hester, in the most cold-blooded manner, let Maude

come to nought trying to explain herself, and Dorothy dared not interpose.

For art as Maude prattled of it for effect, Hester cared nothing; and for art as Hester herself reverenced it, she could make no talk, because she realized that she actually knew little or nothing of it, but only hoped to, hereafter.

It was a relief when Granty returned to Mr. Severn, and started the young ladies off again in a conversation on his fine qualities. They discoursed eloquently until it was time for them to go home; then Maude begged for something to read. With many bewitching flourishes about the tall old bookcase she extracted a copy of "Sakoontala," which she fancied, from something Marion said, was in some way remarkable. "They always do get the newest books that are the best," she reflected; and so, arousing her languid sister, she went home with a story a few thousand years old tucked under her ruffled elbow-sleeve.

"What makes you so sort of savage toward those girls?" asked Granty of Hester. "I don't see any thing amiss. I am sure they seem to want to be very intellectual."

"No: you mean they *want* to *seem* to be very intellectual, and that is just the matter with them, Granty. If they took half the trouble to be genuine that they do to be humbugs, they would be all right.

Now, when they hear of a new book, they buy and read it, if they can, but reviews of it at all events; then they leave it open on the sofa, and entrap callers into speaking of it: so they can air their borrowed ideas. It makes them bores. There is their sister Molly: I like her very much. She is so perfectly natural and truthful to herself, that she is refreshing to talk with, and seems original when she never dreams of being so. Maude was showing me an exquisitely illustrated copy of "The Marble Faun" one day when I was in there, and having raptures over it. Molly coolly declared she had been three weeks trying to read it, and was not one bit interested. If Donatello was a creature with furry ears, why not say so; and, if he was not, what was the use of suggesting that maybe he was: anyway the book bored her. Maude was shocked, because she knew I had said what I thought only a little while before; but Molly did not care for that. They keep their poor mother strained up to such a pitch of would-be intellectuality it is harrowing to behold; and she, in turn, tries to tone up poor Mr. Howell."

"Yes," laughed Marion: "one winter she read him 'Paradise Lost' every evening. One night toward spring he rebelled; but she said, 'Have patience, do Jacob! We have got over the worst of it.' But we will not talk about our neighbors. They are sweet-tempered, pretty girls, and they will 'get over' their art and their artifices."

"Yes," continued Granty, "they are a nice clever family. Mrs. Howell is a splendid housekeeper, and the minister could not have a better boarding-place. I am glad he is over there."

"So am I," said Marion innocently.

CHAPTER VIII.

The Letter Aunt Huldah did not get.

MR. WINTHROP CRAIG sat solitary in the innermost editorial room of "The Phœnix" office. In an outer room the associate editor was blandly, firmly refusing the manuscript of a persistent woman, whose earnest conviction it was that he was blind to the interests of his journal in not accepting her "Parallel between Spenser and Tennyson, with Quotations from Each." She was insisting on seeing "Mr. Craig himself" as an ultimate authority, and the calm associate would not let her. The former gentleman, secure in his retreat, was running over manuscript after manuscript, thrusting each into some pigeon-hole as he finished it; then he began on a pile of letters, reading them with the same expression of patient continuance in well-doing.

The fourth, being opened, disclosed eight neatly-written pages. Too long by far for a business-epistle, it must have been meant for publication; but it was written on each side of every page, as Mr.

Craig noted with disapproval. He smoothed it out, turned to the first sheet, and, behold, it was a letter! A letter to him? He glanced at the first four words, then in amazement turned back to the envelope. Yes, it was to him. He looked to the end; but no name was there. He returned to the four words, "*You dear, neglected creature!*"

Now, the courteous and dignified editor-in-chief of a first-class journal devoted to art, literature, and science, may sometimes, in a purely unprofessional fashion, feel himself socially, or in some tenderer wise, a dear, neglected creature; but it is not when seated in his editorial chair, by any manner of means. Mr. Craig's black eyebrows met, and formed almost a fierce horizontal bar. Again he went back to the last page, and discovered, travelling straight up one side of the paper, in a truly feminine way, the words, "Your loving niece." *Niece!* His only brother died aged six, his one sister a year later, she being ten years old. It was plainly impossible for any niece, no matter how long lost, to arise and call him uncle. Somebody's else niece was writing to some other uncle. The letter, by some inexplicable mistake, had come to him. If it were ever to reach its destination, he must read it. To throw it into his waste-basket might be to bury forever some tidings of weighty import. The handwriting was firm and well formed. The punctuation and paragraphing were as in some article designed for print. With the reflection that the "loving niece" was used to a pen, Mr. Craig began the perusal of the letter.

YOU DEAR, NEGLECTED CREATURE, — It is too unkind that we have kept you so long without news from — *The Spinsterage*, as I want to call our home; but Hester proposes it should be *Happy-Go-Lucky Lodge*. This, however, is not dignified enough to please Granty. Of course you want to know first of her welfare, and will be glad to hear that she was never better. Often I think there is vitality enough in her to stock six lively little old ladies. She gave us a great fright this morning by slipping on a bit of paper, and bumping her head against the door. We bathed it with arnica, and put her to bed, because her eyes ached, and her spine felt queerly, also the back of her head. Hester had been reading one of uncle Jack's books, and said cerebro-spinal meningitis began in that way. However, when Jack came in and told her that Mrs. Wells was in town for a day or two, she arose, and took Dorothy out for an afternoon of formal calls. Dorothy is as busy as ever. I do not know how we could have gotten along after uncle's death without her. His patients were scattered all over the country, you know; his bills were of years' standing, and sometimes his accounts very hard to make up. We tried our best to help her. Hester spent a week making out two bills. One was for an old lady who had chronic rheumatism. She always used to make uncle take his electric machine, and give her "shocks." The other bill was against an old bachelor who had had cataracts taken off his eyes, with long preliminary treatment for other infirmities. Of course, when uncle had performed special operations, he had charged accordingly, and entered it in his day-book; but Hester mixed those two bills up in the most extraordinary manner. They were sent in; and both the old lady and the old gentleman were hopping with indignation. He was charged for an amount of electricity he declared he had never received; and she was shocked more severely than by any battery to learn that her eyes were put down (as Hester said) in uncle's books as "about sightless." The amount charged each was incorrect, of course; and such a time as we had getting it all straightened! To this day, I believe the grumpy old fellow thinks he paid for remedies *she* took; and she imagines that she bore the expenses of *his* ophthalmic operations, although neither paid half they owed. Dorothy has never asked for help since then. She does get along so beautifully with all kinds of people, however, that she never makes enemies, even when stiffly maintaining her rights. Young men and widowers admire her as much as ever; while Hester and I have no "followers whatever," as Bridget O'Flarity sympathetically remarks. Bridget has gone to a wedding to-day. It is just as it used to be when you were here. Granty humors our servant-girls until they soon get to be like death, and have,— "all seasons for their own."

"I am writing very steadily now, because I am doing it with a purpose,— the definite one of earning my bread and jelly; although Hester says we shall never lack it while we live with Granty. She is so thoroughly pious, the Lord will provide for *her;* and she is so particular, he will know she must have plenty, or she will not understand why. I believe Hester is right, for Granty is a wonderfully good little woman. No matter how busy we are, she calls every one of us together in the morning, reads from the Bible, and prays like an inspired Quakeress. Have you never noticed what full, strong, beautifully expressed prayers hers always are, and so often in the finest Scripture language, as if that came first, and was to her most sincere?

"When it comes to household matters, as Thomas à Kempis says, "what" she is "that" she is, "and cannot be another." We tried to enforce upon her daily lessons of economy. We held a council, and decided she must conform more to circumstances. The week after, we held another, and resolved to make circumstances conform to her: it was the easiest way. She must live in a generous way, and have plenty to send to sick ministers, poor neighbors, and so on; then you know it is a necessity of her nature to give tea-parties on the slightest provocation, or none at all.

"Do you think we could tell her she shall not give as liberally as ever to send Christian almanacs to every latitude? No: we bound ourselves never to "pester" that dear little New-England lady with economy as long as she lives, and we will not. Hester paints more than ever nowadays: she has quite a studio. There is a fashion, you know, for panel pictures, — lilies, bird-nests, wild flowers, cat-tails, and little studies of this sort: she paints these exquisitely. However, the domestic wheel would never revolve if Dorothy were not at the hub.

"You ask about little Jack in your last letter. O dear aunt Huldah! How shall we ever bring up a boy? He has the manners of a small savage, with the heart of a wee gentleman. Once a day Granty says, "Spare the rod, and spoil the child;" then Hester cuts a switch, and rings the dinner-bell, which is the signal Jack is wanted. Before he gets here, Granty remembers he is a peculiar child, and cannot be dealt with severely: so he only asks about the switch with innocent interest, and gets a "turn-over" Bridget has baked for him. We are all through house-cleaning, and the old home never looked prettier. I must be getting old-fashioned myself; for our rooms grow more attractive to me every year. I used to think the solid tables and great chairs were heavy; but I like it all now, — the great andirons, the rugs, fire-screens, and queer china on the sideboards. Hester says it is only because we are coming back into the latest fashion. Well, I often wonder if three girls ever came up in a cosier corner of the earth than we did in ours. How Granty used to worry because I would not practise "The White Cockade," and be "musical," but would hide in the trees to read "The Vicar of Wakefield"! Do you remember the time uncle Jack let Hester stay out of school to paint a landscape, with three dreadful Zouaves in firemen's breeches, on the inside of the barn-door? We do not miss uncle Jack less, as the days go by, in many ways: in others we do. A heavy step now in the hall does not make me expect his hearty laugh, or the frolic with Jack. When I look down the shaded street, and see a broad-shouldered old man coming, I have ceased to think it is he. I am getting used to the thought that he can never come in jesting, or come in weary, or come any way at all. But, while there is any home here, he is in one way within it, and always will be. It is curious how we regulate things by his ideas. Hester is never sharp to his tedious old women who come for medicine yet: she lets them waste her time, and Dorothy makes them tea. We are never tempted to be short-suffering or uncharitable; but we remember how comically gentle he was to everybody weak, or ignorant, or lacking, how he was "patient with fools." A little corner of his big mantle even seems to rest on little Jack. He brings all the lame dogs in the street to Hester to doctor.

"But dearie me, what a letter this is! Jack told me somebody said to him recently, "If your aunt Marion is an authoress, her conversation must be *improving.*" He answered that may be it was improving; but he did not know any thing had *ailed* it. Something "ails" this letter, — a very great lack of connection; but you will not be critical. You are a precious, good-natured old lady. ["Am I, though?" ejaculated Mr. Craig.]

"I cannot tell you much that is new; but there is a fine minister, I have heard, settled over the old First Church. He boards at the Howells's across the road: Granty has met him, and Dorothy also. Oh! I send you a photograph of myself, taken not long ago, not very good. When are you coming for your summer visit? I must tell you that Hester has bought a *cow;* and we fear that much learning, from reading works bearing on the care of that domestic animal, has made her mad. She announced yesterday that good authorities advocated the milking of cows three times a day. Granty said never while *she* lived should such a thing be done. If she had no regard for the cow, she had too much self-respect to experiment in a way that looked so outrageously mean. The supper-bell is ringing! I embrace you, as the French say. Good-by.

Your loving niece,

MARION.

"Phew!" exclaimed the editor of "The Phœnix." "You embrace me, do you! And I — I cannot tell you how to bring up Jack, or even advise you about Hester's cow! I"—

Out dropped the photograph, and Mr. Craig rescued it promptly from the floor. The associate-editor put his head in the door, and asked a question. The chief composed himself, but did not look around until the head was removed.

If Marion, as she sat that day at dinner, serenely pouring cream over her strawberries, could have beheld this scene in the distant city!— Her letter under the broad palm of a total stranger; her photograph, for the moment, poised on a horrid inkstand, in the shape of a horned toad, while the stranger carefully studied it (the face, not the toad) with the eye of a phrenologist.

"Fine head," he murmured, "about twenty-five I presume — good nose and chin — forehead of a woman with ideas — looks too grave to have written the letter — should have thought her style would have been grave to melancholy. No! there is life enough in the eyes. Well, my loving niece, what the deuse shall I do with you and with your revelation of domestic affairs! I wish I knew the way to your Happy-Go-Lucky Lodge! It must be a merry old place, with so many funny women in it; but I cannot return your letter."

He folded it carefully again, the photograph in it, and laid it away in a private drawer. A few moments later, and he was in the midst of his professional cares again, had forgotten the letter, and was only dimly conscious that the editor in the outer room was metaphorically wrestling with a gentleman, whose article, if only it could be published, would be a death-blow to Herbert Spencer. The obtuse editor, having himself no designs on the latter's life, would not be persuaded to take the fatal article in charge.

CHAPTER IX.

Jack makes a Friend.

ONE day there came a letter from aunt Huldah. Dorothy opened and read it to the family. It began thus: —

DEAR ONES ALL, — I do not see what makes you so very long silent. If it were not such an effort for me to write letters, I should have written before to know if any thing was the matter. ["The unreasonable old lady!" interposed Marion. "I wrote her an endless amount of family matters."] Mr. Pepperfield has not been well this summer, but is now. I have been busy all the time, and now want a play-spell. I want to see you all, and write to propose something which I hope will be agreeable. What would Marion say to coming to Ingleside and staying a few weeks, while I go and visit you? I cannot leave poor Pepperfield alone with the servants, and Marion might enjoy the change. She will have nothing to do, but to pour his coffee, and to see that the girls do not break my new decorated china. She can write without interruption; and we have pleasant neighbors, if she wishes company. She might bring Jack with her: he can roam the woods with her. Write and tell me if she will come: if so, and you wish me, shall I do any shopping for you in the city? I shall go in soon.

Your affectionate aunt,
HULDAH PEPPERFIELD.

"Go by all means, Marion!" said Granty briskly. "It will do you good, and I want to see Huldah very much. If I were in your place, I would go right off this week. Is there any thing to hinder?"

The old lady liked changes and excitement of this sort. Marion knew at once she had best go; but fortunately the plan had nothing disagreeable about it: so she answered, "I will go next Tuesday."

"And I," said Granty, "shall sit right down, and write to Huldah to come at once. She can leave Mr. Pepperfield over Sunday alone, I am sure. And now, girls, we have so much to do!"

She began to tell them what this "much" was; and Hester, after hearing, went to her studio, and turned all the half-painted Scudders with their faces to the wall. She could not paint for several days to come.

One uninitiated into Granty's modes of procedure might not have understood why the coming of one woman and the going of another necessitated the turning wrong side out of all the closets, and the airing of innumerable clothes on ropes in the backyard, why the woodshed-roof must be at once shingled, and all odd jobs, in season and out, attended to with as much precipitancy as if placid aunt Huldah were an investigating committee of some sort; but so it was, and the next few days were busy ones. The lawn was shaved, the cistern cleaned out. Dorothy preserved fruit, and Marion made a travelling-dress. Hester continued her course of reading on cows, and talked with neighbors in regard to keeping hens. Milk had naturally suggested eggs; and Pete, who had a turn for architecture, wished to build a hen-house in his hours of ease. Granty pervaded the entire premises with the alacrity of a wilful breeze that has a good deal to do, and does not mind in the least whom it ruffles, or what it displaces, as it goes its way. She kept them all busy until afternoon each day; then she stepped into the phaeton, and, with one of them for a companion, took the air. Old Mortality would meander over the surrounding country, sometimes stopping, apparently better to hear the conversation, and always agitating her mind more or less, as to which of his legs, "fore or aft," were the weak ones. Two of them must be; else why did he, ever and anon, seem inclined to kneel reverently with his front ones, or to sit serenely down in the rear.

Well, one evening a little later in the week, aunt Huldah arrived. She bustled in, and was not tired, but found the cool supper-room "delightful." She had not been hungry; but the hot biscuit were "delicious." So she ate and drank and chatted. She let Jack drag in her trunk then, and hint that it had better be opened. This being done, she produced a new dress all around, a white cap for Granty, a bow and arrows for Jack, even a gorgeous pin and earrings for Miss O'Flarity. She made Hester tell her what she was painting, and instructed Marion how to make the forsaken Pepperfield happy in her absence. She listened eagerly to Granty, and heard portions of Jack's harrowing tale of how Buttercup would have been choked on a turnip, had not Bridget gone down her throat after it as far as her (Bridget's) armpit. In short, aunt Huldah was one of them, and therefore was soon at home.

It began to rain Saturday, and rained until Tuesday morning; then the sun shone out gloriously, and all the family were actively interested in getting Marion started. Granty would never allow one of them to travel without a lunch; for all the "food at stations was unwholesome:" so Marion had one put up for her large enough for a man of an "unbounded stomach," to say nothing of a woman with a little boy. Then, although Marion was never ill in her life, Granty would not be gainsaid, but, with Hester's help, put up a compressed apothecary's shop for her, — camphor, brandy, laudanum, aconite, Jamaica ginger, — and was going right on, when Marion entreated her to desist. Did they wish to have her, in case of an accident, published as a vender of quack medicine?

"Now, my child, don't hurry to get on or off while the cars are in motion, and do be careful of yourself," said Granty, when Marion, having locked her trunk, sat down to draw on the pretty gray gloves that matched her dress so well. "And write as soon as you get there! If you get sick, send for some of us right away," continued the old lady. "You know you are naturally heedless. — Is there any malaria in Ingleside, Huldah?"

"I don't know of any," answered that lady placidly.

"And Jack, — oh, dear! I feel dreadfully about that child's going! Have you got the gargle for his throat, in case he needs it?"

"Yes, Granty."

"And his thick flannel shirts, if it should get cold?"

"Yes, every thing of the sort."

"You will see that he doesn't run the streets on Sunday?"

"Why, of course, Granty."

"He never has had the scarlet-fever," she remarked suggestively.

"Perhaps I might get him exposed to it," answered Marion roguishly.

"Oh, no! not for any thing, Marion! And you won't get absorbed in your writing, and let him get out on the roof to play, or go following fire-engines to the water, and be drowned, will you? I have always expected that he would some day go where they are blasting rocks, and be blown all to pieces. I try, when he is at home, to keep these things in my mind."

"I promise you, Granty, to take the best kind of care of him," returned Marion.

She sank into silence, but awoke again, to add, "If you put him at the back side of a bed, he will throw all the clothes off, and take his death of cold."

"Then I will not put him there."

"But, if he lies in the front, he will surely tumble out. Oh, I don't know how you ever will get along with him anyway! You mark my words for it, if he eats cheese or smoked halibut for his supper, he will talk all night."

"Take good care of my husband," interposed aunt Huldah.

"Carriage at the gate!" shouted Jack, who looked like a sweet little dandy in a new suit of navy-blue, and a sailor hat.

"I do hope this long storm has not made trouble on the railroad," was Granty's last exclamation; but the driver cut the good-bys short, and whirled the travellers away to the station. The first part of their journey was uneventful. They rode in a drawing-room car until three in the afternoon; and all the passengers were so uniformly genteel and monotonously well-behaved, Jack would have found it dull, but for the luncheon and the ice-cream bought him, under protest, by Marion. What if the colored man did take it from car to car, with the coal-dust flying over it, and, it may be, do strange, unlawful things to it in the mysterious regions from whence he bore it hither? It *looked* clean, Jack argued. At three o'clock they changed trains, and, getting into a common car, were more entertained. Here their fellow-creatures were like needles in a paper, — well assorted. A happy Dutchman, who looked like a priest, but needs must have been a married man, sat across from them, with his stolid *frau* and three younglings. One of these was a boy, who ate Bologna sausages and drank beer from a basket that must have connected, in some unseen manner, with a grocery, and continually replenished; for out of it the second, a snarling girl, drew gingerbread baked in pie-crust, while baby (very unpleasant to look upon) was supplied with unlimited milk. Even the parents occasionally stirred up odors of garlic and unfamiliar cheese from the same repository. In front of Marion was a gentleman absorbed in a newspaper. His shoulders were broad, his overcoat handsome. The back of his head being covered with abundant and somewhat curly hair, Jack signified his intention of giving it "a little twist, you know;" for what purpose only a boy could have told. The idea was not carried out. A little farther off were the bride and groom (without which no train ever runs), and behind them, much amused thereat, three school-girls. Loudest of all, in a full tide of mutual confidences, were two matrons. Marion was pleased to learn that the one in a brown bonnet trimmed with green grapes had a daughter "splendidly" educated, if her "ma did keep boarders in order to fetch it." She had a piano that cost "four hundred, and not new at that." It was also interesting, if sad, to be informed that said daughter had married a "scalawag." "Yes," affirmed she of the artificial grapes, "after all my pains, she came back on my hands, and he too. I have the feelings of a mother, and I long to pick up a chair, and throw at his head."

The second matron, above the roar and rattle of the car, explained that her son was a night watchman in a city hospital. The doctors wanted him once or twice to sell his blood for transfusion into sick patients, at two dollars a time. He did so, but, being "one of your particular sort," insisted it should go into "no poor trash." Just as the passengers were getting interested in the young man, she dropped her voice, and they only heard from the mother once more. About dark, as she left the car, they heard her say, that, as for her, she "would not give flour pancakes stomach-room."

Marion expected to get to Ingleside about nine o'clock; but at six they began to lose time. The train made frequent stops, with many shrieks, much ringing of the bell, and seasons of going backward. Granty's fears were for once prophetic. The storm had made bad work on the railroad. Jack informed himself that the track was washed away in places, and they feared it would be quite under water farther on. The ladies bestirred themselves to look out of the window; the men to go and question somebody. Confused murmurs arose from parties who had expected friends to meet them. The gentleman whose back hair had attracted Jack put down his paper, and stretched himself. In so doing, one arm was spread out on the back of his seat, and the broad palm of his hand dropped invitingly open. In a flash, Jack's fat little paw met it, and gave it just the friendly shake it might have expected, but certainly did not. Marion could have shaken Jack, in turn; but it was too late. The stranger turned, after a glance at Jack, gave a genial laugh, and exclaimed, "Happy to meet you, sir! Would you like to read my newspaper?"

"If it is full of murders, aunt Marion won't let me.

The last one I read, she said I must stop, or I would have a hanging of my own some day."

"That was wise in her. Don't you want to come over here?"

As Jack was balancing on the back of the seat, it was certainly courteous to invite him farther, and equally so to prevent Marion from thinking he wished to entrap her into conversation. Jack, with one thorough searching of the gentleman's face, found it a good, masterful countenance. Thereupon his red stockings and funny cropped head vanished over the dividing line, he explaining as he went, "She wants me to read those Christian papers about bad boys. I believe she means *me* when she reads them out loud. Granty does it Sundays."

"Oh! I don't think you are a bad boy."

"Aunt Dorothy (I have got four — no, five aunts), — she is surprised I am not worse; for I have not prayed for myself in *ever* so long. I begin, you know, with the great-aunts, and I stop to think — one of them has got a husband — I would get to myself, if I didn't get sleepy first. Dorothy found it out sort o' by accident: I s'pose she was listening to me."

"I have heard of people who never prayed for anybody but themselves. Your way is better; but I think it is too generous."

"I have been taken care of, though; being in the family, I suppose. That woman over there looks like our Bridget. She is awfully comical. I asked her if she wanted to go back to Ireland, and she said, 'Dade, thin! No Irish dog shall ever bark at me.'"

"That was a poetical way of saying she should stay in America."

"Poetical!" echoed Jack, adding quickly, "she has a beau, a cousin she calls him: they always do, Granty says. She got mad at him last night: she said, 'He had a nose on him, and I had a nose on me: he took his turned-up nose away wid him, and I kaped me turned-up nose behint.'"

The gentleman looking mildly interested, Jack went on, "What do you think she calls the theological seminary?"

"I cannot imagine."

"Well, she says it is a 'zoölogical cemetery.'"

"Not so bad," said the gentleman. "But what are we stopping here for, so long?" He arose and went to the door. Marion took that chance to tell Jack not to talk about his aunts, or any thing pertaining thereto. A man came through the car, and lighted the lamps, also giving the dismal information that the track along by the river was all under water, and they might be delayed hours on the way. The gentleman, returning from the door, found acquaintances, and stopped to chat with them. Men with lanterns hurried back and forth through the cars. Passengers grumbled, predicted disaster, or "guessed" there was no danger, according to their sex and disposition. At nine o'clock they were far from Ingleside. Marion was very grateful for Granty's nice luncheon. It had given Jack something wherewith to comfort his drooping spirits. When the last cake vanished, he curled himself up, and went to sleep. Marion must have dozed also; for it was midnight when she came wide awake to find herself cold and uncomfortable. Through her window the flickering lights shone on a gloomy expanse of water. She heard its plash against the car-wheels below. A sharp wind blew in when the opposite doors were opened, and everybody else in the car seemed to have awakened with her to acute discomfort. A crosser, more dismal, cold, and unsympathetic set of people, could hardly be imagined. Jack arose, blinking, from under Marion's wrap, and asked, "Are we *there?*"

"No, Jack: we are not anywhere in particular; and I do not like it. My heart is in my mouth."

"It is not," he returned, with decision. "If it was, you would have to spit it out. And it is too big, anyway," he added, not by way of compliment, but because of Hester's correct physiological teachings. "Are you afraid, aunt Marion?"

"A little."

"Do you think God will take care of us?"

"Oh, certainly, Jack!"

"Then what do you worry for? Here, put your shawl on."

"I do not want it, Jack. You will be cold."

The small man wrapped it around her with affectionate fury; then he asked if the last cake had gone up. It had gone down, so he said it was no matter. In the same philosophic spirit, the gentleman whom Jack admired was going up and down the car, making things more endurable. He shut the draughts that were chilling everybody. He jested as if they were on a steamer, and, peering out, declared he saw the Irish coast. He quieted the fears of a feeble old woman, and found her a more comfortable seat. He advised a sulky acquaintance to take up a collection for the yellow-fever sufferers: it would make them all feel better.

"That man is a gentleman," thought Marion, after quietly watching him. "He loses no dignity, while he brightens up everybody. — Where are you, Jack? Come back!"

The youngster was careering to the door to look out on the face of the waters. Mindful of Granty's charges, she called him; but he did not hear her. In a minute the gentleman marched him back, sat down with him on his knees, and said, "I have heard of you, little chap, in a book wherein it was written, years ago, —

> "How could you keep down your mirth
> When the floods were on the earth,
> When from all your drowning kin
> Good old Noah took you in?
> In the very ark, no doubt,
> You went frolicking about,
> Never keeping in your mind
> Drowned monkeys left behind."

"Oh! I have heard that before: there is more of it. — You read it to me once; didn't you, aunt Marion?"

The gentleman, turning, said to the latter, —

"Isn't it a treasure of a book for children? It has gone out of fashion; but there are no prettier ballads in literature for children than some of Mary Howitt's of birds and bees and flowers."

"Yes; aunt Marion used to read them often to me. What time do you suppose we shall get into Ingleside? Do you know uncle John Pepperfield?" put in Jack.

Before Marion could stop him from the questions, he had them out, and was answered: "I live at Ingleside, and I know Mr. Pepperfield well. We play a great many games of chess together. I am glad I know where you are going; for, should Mr.

Pepperfield not understand about the delay, he may suppose you are not coming. To arrive after midnight, and meet no friends, would be very unpleasant. Now I can easily find you a carriage."

Marion thanked him. Jack began, "Aunt Pepperfield is at our house, and we"—

Some influence just then exerted caused him to become reticent, to look out of the window, and amuse himself watching for sharks. After an hour more of hitching forward, and jerking back, of starting and of stopping, the lights of Ingleside appeared. When they left the car, it was to find uncle Pepperfield, with much anxiety and a little lantern, scurrying about the platform. The gentleman ran and secured him for them, then courteously bowed himself into the darkness.

CHAPTER X.

The Editor of "The Phœnix."

THERE could not be a more charming home than aunt Pepperfield's. The house, a pretty, modern cottage, had airy rooms with one-paned windows, whose dark casings framed exquisite landscapes. The house stood on a hill overlooking little hamlets, a broad, shining river, and the great city, softened by distance. In the rear was a flourishing garden, where uncle Pepperfield, in a battered straw hat, was forever finding something to dig or train or prune or plant, — a garden that had no prim end, but, getting enough of flowers and vegetables, rolled itself on in velvety turf, until it tumbled over into the merriest little brook imaginable. It scrambled up on the other side, and crept to the edge of a grove of thick trees, almost like a forest. Ingleside was properly not a village at all, but a beautiful spot, where people of taste and moderate means could enjoy rural life, yet be near the city, — a place where families of great wealth could put up warlike castles of mixed architecture to serve as peaceful country-seats.

Marion and Jack were very happy here. The cares of the former were light. She presided over the decorated china; saw Mr. Pepperfield off to town in good clothes, or to the garden in old ones; made a tour of the rooms; cared for the pictures, vases, the multitudinous tidies and mats aunt Huldah delighted in; then took papers and pen into the piazza, that overlooked miles of land and water, — of woods where each tree was having its outline pricked out in scarlet or yellow on the hitherto monotonous green of summer. The outlook quickened Marion's fancies, and she blackened an incredible amount of paper. The afternoons she gave to Jack. They roamed the grove, and made an aquarium by the brook. A gay young lady might have found it dull: Marion did not, and so assured Mr. Pepperfield whenever he proposed to invite guests, or to take her to the city for variety.

One evening he exclaimed, as he put down his cup, "Upon my word, you ought to know some of our friends! There is a capital chap who comes here frequently; but I have not set eyes on him lately. He is one of your sort too."

"Why? Is he a little old maid?"

"Nonsense! You don't belong to the sisterhood,

and can't for a dozen years. The crinkles must get out of your hair, the twinkles out of your eyes, and the red off your cheeks, before you read your title clear," said uncle Pepperfield, who was a gallant old gentleman in the main. "Besides, there are no old maids nowadays, only a few left over from the last century, hidden away in corners. Bless 'em! They ought to have as much honor paid to them as folks are paying to old spinning-wheels and other precious relics. No: the women who don't get married in these days know the reason why, and other folks generally are ready to believe it is a good one. Some make themselves so smart it is likely they were predestinated to just that smartness, and are as great a success as if they had married."

"Uncle Pepperfield," cried Marion, "once utter those sentiments in public, and you are a marked man. Some progressive club will elect you speaker. Aunt Huldah will have you snatched from domestic life to be a champion of women in general, of maidens in particular. I thank you as an individual, and will not expose your opinions. But how were you going to show that your friend was an old maid?"

"I never said a word about old maids: you began it yourself. Tender point, after all, I guess," continued Mr. Pepperfield. "I only meant that he was literary. He writes, he edits a paper, he makes public speeches. He is a good fellow; a confirmed old bachelor, — disappointed, it may be, or perhaps he has not met her."

Mr. Pepperfield emptied his cup, ate all his peaches and cream, then sat and smiled suggestively.

"What is it?" asked Marion innocently.

"Suppose he should come here; suppose each of you should say the same thing" —

"About the weather, perhaps — why, that would be very tame" —

"Suppose," persisted Mr. Pepperfield, "that simultaneous expression should be *veni, vidi, vici*, pronounced, of course, *wany, wedy, weky*. Would it not be nice, Marion? Two pens with but a single inkstand! You could give each other hints when hard pressed for topics, and buy your foolscap together, at a discount. Shall I ask him to tea?"

"No," returned Marion, not to be teased. "Please don't endanger our happiness by asking him. I want my inkstand all to myself. We should quarrel."

"Very well: he will come sooner or later of his own accord; then let him remember what Homer says, 'No man of woman born, coward or brave, can shun his destiny.' In the mean time I want *you* to appreciate my classical allusions. I am making dreadful efforts to be fit company for an authoress."

.

"I thought something queer ailed you," laughed Marion; "but I beg of you not to distress yourself any more. Are you going into the city to-morrow, uncle Pepperfield?"

"I am. Will you and Jack go with me?"

"We will. I have some little things to attend to, and Jack wants to see the sights," answered Marion, as they arose from the table.

On the day following, the three went into town by an early train. Mr. Pepperfield planned to meet Marion later in the day, and left her for a few hours to her own devices. She went to picture-galleries, art-rooms, and bookstores first, then to a variety-shop to buy bits of lace, ribbon, and pretty trifles that do not find their way into the country. All the morning she was conscious of a large envelope in her pocket. She had sent many like it by mail; but this unstamped one made her uneasy: it even spoiled the dainty lunch she took with Jack about noon. The fact was, that Marion had resolved to carry an article in person to an editor. All these previous years she had kept herself out of sight; but, now that she had undertaken to write as a means of support, it seemed best to do it in the most business-like way. If she went directly to the editor for whom she intended this article, she could inform herself on several points she wished to understand, and that better than she could do by writing to him. She had once before designed an article for this same editor, but had condemned it later as unsuitable. It was to him she had by chance sent a remarkable chronicle of the Prescott family affairs, although this was certainly *not* one of the many thoughts in her mind.

"Jack," she exclaimed, as they emerged from a candy-shop, his mouth and pocket equally distended with sweets, "I am going to an editor's office: you must be as still as a mouse if you go."

"Going to sit with your head in iron pinchers, and leave a negative behind you?" asked Jack, with misty ideas of a photographer's establishment.

"I may leave a negative behind me," she murmured, glancing at a plate-glass window, which reflected a little figure in a gray silk, with a bunch of pink asters in the belt, veil and gloves to match. It was pleasant to think, that if she was literary, and was going to an editor, and did have a manuscript in her pocket, she was not like a caricature, with cotton gloves and green veil, with long nose and spectacles. Her manuscript was not poetry; and, if he did not want it, other editors would. This she knew by experience, and it put courage into her. Presently she saw, on a great gilded sign, "Office of The Phœnix." Mounting a long flight of stairs, she entered a large room, with smaller ones all about it, and various men at various desks scattered here and there in a bewildering way. Any one of them might be Mr. Craig. But a boy passing out informed her he was in the most remote room, and she could "go right in." She left Jack in the first seat; and feeling very small and very presumptuous, and as if every one of those probably very highly gifted men sprinkled about the place knew what she had in her pocket, and that it was not half as good as she had supposed it to be, she went on and straight into the little room. It held quantities of papers in piles and racks, also a big desk, a big man in a big chair, with his broad shoulders turned to her, and one smaller chair, into which she sank when he turned, and asked her to be seated. He wrote a moment longer, called a boy, sent him with a paper into space, and then wheeled about toward Marion. At one glance she recognized her fellow-traveller, the aristocratic Mark Tapley, who had come out so well that dismal night on the cars. Not that he looked guilty of jollity: he was editorial gravity itself.

"How glad I am I left Jack outside!" thought Marion, when she saw he did not recognize her. Jack would have greeted him like a long-lost brother; and he might have thought she was making that meeting, and the fact of his being Mr. Pepperfield's acquaintance, a passport to his favor. Well for her she did not dream at the moment that this was the very friend of whom her uncle had talked: she would hardly have been so serene in stating her errand. As it was, she talked with the clearness and precision of a bell that does not give one unnecessary stroke. Mr. Craig told her that the article, if left, would receive due attention; that many well-written articles were offered them that they could not publish. He gave her full answers to all her questions, and was very courteous, although his eyes returned to his work in a way that was somewhat suggestive. Her errand accomplished, she arose to go; and, with a pleasant smile, he looked directly in her face. She saw at once a puzzled expression flit across his, and fade out. She knew he was wondering where he had seen her, and was secretly amused to think she could tell him if she chose. Could she have done it? He had actually seen little more than her veil in the cars; but that very moment there was a photograph of her folded in her letter in the desk at which he sat. He bowed very graciously as she retired, and in two moments had forgotten her existence. Jack greeted her as if she had been gone a year; and they went gayly forth to meet Mr. Pepperfield.

When they were comfortably seated in the cars for the return home, Marion said, "Uncle, do you remember, that, the night I arrived in Ingleside, a gentleman helped us off the cars, and found you? Well, he is the editor of 'The Phœnix,' isn't he? Does he live there?"

"Certainly. Why, *that* is Craig! Well, I declare! if you had not met him already, after all my planning!"

"Yes; and I have seen him again to-day. Now, I beg of you not to ask him to tea while he is sitting in judgment on my ten-page article."

"You need not fear: it would not have the least influence with him. I might feed him on ambrosia, and introduce him to Venus herself: he would eat one, and admire the other; but, if Venus offered him, next day, a poor poem, he would not accept it for love nor money. You will get justice done you, and nothing more."

At this point Jack wished to buy the valuable jewel supposed to be embedded in a dime package of gum-drops, and the purchase turned the conversation to other matters.

That evening Marion received the following letter from Hester:—

DEAR MARION,—We are all well; but some of us ought to take time to tell you so, or you will worry. We have just recovered from a tea-party, which we had very severely. Granty said there were a few friends of aunt Pepper's that we must invite to tea, and that it would be neighborly to have the Howells and the minister over there. Dorothy agreed, of course, and we began to plan for about enough people to sit around the table with all its leaves in; but we are simple. We might have known that one of Granty's incipient tea-parties goes immediately to work like Æsop's bull-frog, and swells and swells, until the grand explosion is that of a very big thing indeed. Ours was, I assure you. But it was very pleasant, and every one came who was invited, — about forty in all. Granty said the outer kitchen-door and the back-steps must be repainted first. Dorothy thought it unnecessary, as the guests came in after dark, at the front-door. But we had it done, and they look nicely, — at least they did. You know the dog's trick of scratching to be let in? Well, the painter said he must be kept from it, and I tied him to the table-leg in the office; but Granty, going in there, let him loose. She said he looked as if his "feelings were hurt." Mine were; for he ran directly, and rubbed his nose and paws all over the fresh paint. I tried to remove his tracks myself by repainting with my tube colors; but it made me think of Maude Howells's remarks to Mr. Severn about "large aims, and inadequacy of expression." It is a pretty way she has of talking of art to him, and quite harmless; only I wonder she can enjoy it. She chirped away sweetly about "pre-Raphaelites and impressionists, sects in art, painters' techniques, and æstheticism." He looked at her with comical attention, and I was wicked enough to wonder what new book it was this time. Marion, you need not buy me the cashmere dress I spoke of having. I have spent the money. When I came to painting the last little fright of a Scudder girl, I resolved to take the price of her head, so to speak, and get the new dress; but I have had to buy up, instead, about five hundred old relatives. Maybe you do not understand the obligation. I did not at first; but I have bought them all the same.

Do you remember a fellow named Dusenberry, who was forever writing to uncle Jack to find out about some branch of the Coxe family, or the Wiggins or the Higgins who "intermarried," always ending his letters with, "And please answer *who* and *where* and *what* and *when;* your loving cousin, Dusenberry"? Well, it seems that for forty years he has been making out the genealogy of the Prescott family, — getting up a big book. It is done; and he writes that it will be of the "profoundest interest" to us; that uncle would certainly have taken it (and paid ten dollars); that he considers the price of it, therefore, a debt of honor which we will be glad to discharge. Now, if it were on the side of the "New-England" ancestors, I would like to know every thing about the people of whom we have so many pictures and relics; but for the rest — Uncle Jack used to say he "would not give a sixpence for the whole shake of them," up to his contemporaries, whom he liked, of course. We talked it over, and vowed we would not have it; then we remembered uncle Jack's ways. We knew he would have laughed at the loving cousin for a pertinacious pest, and sent the money. So I took a last sad look at De Soto discovering the Mississippi, on the face of my new greenback, and mailed it to Dusenberry. To-day a mighty tome arrived, bound in bright magenta cloth, which looks dreadfully on our table-covers, and is too large for the book-case. Would it not be quite appropriate to use it for a pedestal to the family skeleton, and leave it there, with the "old associations" that Mrs. Ruggles palmed off on us? Write and tell us what you and Jack are doing to amuse yourselves. Tell uncle Pepperfield he cannot have aunt Huldah yet: we want her several weeks longer. She is enjoying herself very much. I must tell you how she took Old Mortality, and went all alone for a drive, one day soon after she came. He went very well until she was about seven miles from home, then he fell into that agonizing drag, drag, as if protesting against the cruelty of expecting him to move. She did not understand, and fancied he was sick: so she stopped at various farmhouses, and had him examined. At last one man brought her a long slim lath, and told her to slap him the whole length of his body, if he did not care for the whip. She did not get home at sunset, and Granty was wild with fright, declaring he had *run away* with her. I had to borrow Mr. Howells's horse and phaeton about eight o'clock, and go in search of them with bandages, hartshorn, and brandy; with a lantern, too, to find them, if mangled by the wayside. I met them crawling into town by the toll-gate; and aunt Huldah, for once, was not singing a hymn. I believe she longed to do something else that begins with "s."

Dorothy will write you when she gets time. Perhaps she will forget to tell you that Mr. Jerry Scudder comes to bother me about his family photographs much oftener than necessary, and always asks for her on some pretext or other.

THURSDAY MORNING. — I forgot to send this letter Tuesday; for, before I finished it, we had a sudden call from Mrs. Howells. A great party of relatives had come unexpectedly to visit her; and, compress her family as she might, there were still, as in the old puzzle, too many people for the beds. Would we take Mr. Severn here to board for a week or two? He was "no more trouble than a little kitten." She might have known, if he had been as much trouble as a whole menagerie of mature tiger-cats, Granty's neighborliness would have been equal to the demand. Well, Mr. Severn came, and we have put him into your room. The first rainy day he drifted into the office, and Granty said he might as well use it for a study as to be going back and forth between the two houses. Even in these three days, he has filled the office, so to speak, with literary sandwiches; for between every two books on the body there now seems to be one on the soul. Not that he is pushing in the least: I like him now I have seen him. Last evening we were together, alone in the parlor, and I forgot him entirely; but he must have been refreshed by silence and reflection; for the next day he told Molly Howells I was "extremely sensible." If he has a capacity for silence, we will agree beautifully. Marion, if Jack has the croup, give him the remedies marked No. 1; for simple sore throat, No. 2. If you are not sure send for a doctor immediately. Now good-by.

Yours,
HESTER PRESCOTT.

"Well, well!" exclaimed Marion. "Hester likes the minister, does she? He had better go back to the Howellses as soon as possible! Getting interested in interesting clergymen is a common and well-known weakness. I hope this one has not dyspepsia or chronic hoarseness. Hester never can see a human being ailing in any way, and let the creature alone."

CHAPTER XI.

Dorothy and the Photographs.

DOROTHY PRESCOTT was a person who had to make herself agreeable, unless there was a well-defined necessity that she should be otherwise. She infused such *bonhomie* into the dryest affairs of life, that old grumblers, crusty officials, disobliging workmen, anybody in contact with her, lost rapidly stiffness, grumpiness, and gravity. She did not feel more interest in her fellow-creatures than did Hester or Marion; but she elicited at first more confidence and sympathy. She found out people's vulnerable points, and attacked them with gay yet kindly audacity: she knew her power, but never abused it. One day during Marion's absence she was quietly sewing, when Hester appeared in the library, with the entire collection of the Scudders, all finished, and ready for removal. Mrs. Scudder, done in a cloud, was greatly improved: indeed, no fault could be found with any of the family, unless one objected to the original design of their faces or figures, for which, certainly, Hester could not be held accountable.

"I am so glad you are through with them!" exclaimed Dorothy. "Now he will stop coming here."

"I doubt that," said Hester. "You have been too polite to him."

"*I!* Aren't you ashamed to say that?"

"Yes, *you!* If you had not listened to his talk about the farm, he would not have brought that jug of maple sirup as a present to Granty. He asked me last week if we had plenty of garden 'sass' on the place. If there is not a damper put on him, he will come courting, as Mrs. Nickelby's old gentleman did, by throwing cucumbers over the garden-wall; and it will all be your fault."

"Yes, Dorothy: you have done very wrong if you have trifled with him," put in Granty severely. "He is a good, clever man; he attends church regularly: and I would not have his feelings hurt for any thing."

"Nor I, Granty. Shall I encourage him? Would you like him for a nephew?"

"Dorothy, you are not a chit of a girl to be flirting. Treat him courteously."

"So I have, and Hester does not like it. Now, what if he comes after the pictures are taken away?"

"The pictures are neither here nor there," said Granty, with the beautiful irrelevancy peculiar to her when too closely questioned.

Meanwhile Hester was decorating the room. Mr. Scudder smiled from the mantel; Mrs. Scudder hovered over the candelabra; the youthful Scudders stared from as many brackets and convenient nooks. She had just placed them when Granty left the room; and soon after Miss O'Flarity let in Mr. Scudder himself.

"You are just in time to see all the pictures together," said Hester; "and you can take them home to-day if you wish. The varnish is quite dry now."

"Oh, my! Aren't they a lot of them?" said he, beginning at his own, and going around as at an exhibition worthy of all attention.

"Do you think mine is good?" he asked soon, turning shyly to Dorothy.

"Yes: I think it an excellent likeness."

He went on, looking pleased, and bestowed approving glances on his offspring. Coming to Mrs. Scudder, he ejaculated, "She as was, and is no more!"

The tone of real feeling had the effect of keeping Dorothy's risibles under control.

"I have a box that will hold them all, and keep them from rubbing together," continued Hester. "I will get it, and pack them, if you wish."

"Thank you! I have my buggy at the gate: I can take them as well as not."

Hester left the room, and was detained a long time.

Dorothy noticed, with a little uneasiness, that Mr. Scudder appeared relieved at her departure.

"She as was, and is no more," he repeated, then suddenly dropped into a chair near Dorothy's own. "And, because she is no more, her place is vacant."

By the ominous tremor in the worthy man's voice, Dorothy was sure, that, in a matrimonial sense, he was about to "leap;" and she as quickly resolved that he should "look" first, and save himself from the act. She broke out in sympathetic cheeriness, "Yes; and you are very lonely. You ought, Mr. Scudder, for your own comfort and the children's, to marry again. There are so many nice girls in the country around here! You ought never to think of marrying anybody but a farmer's daughter; for no town-bred girl could oversee that beautiful great dairy and all your farmwork of the house. You need a stirring, capable woman that understands that perfectly. I don't myself know what that work is to describe it: I never spent two days on a farm in my life. I"—

Dorothy was at a loss now to "narrow in to a close," as speakers say. She only wanted to save his pride, encourage him to marry — somebody else, and let him see the vanity of his present efforts. But it was not easy to demonstrate her unfitness for a position that had not been offered to her.

"What you say is true, Miss Prescott. The house wants a lady about it to keep things ship-shape, and to teach the youngsters better manners. Coming here lately, and seeing how nice and genteel things are where women-folks manage, I thought" — Mr. Scudder gasped — "I thought maybe — maybe — there were so many of you here, one could be spared as well as not. And you" —

"Oh, don't tease us, Mr. Scudder, about being three spinsters, as uncle Jack used to! You see, we grew up very independent, and feel as if we all belonged together. I don't suppose one of us would think of leaving the rest. But there is not much danger of our being asked," rattled on Dorothy hypocritically. "Everybody knows we are one and inseparable. But it is *you* we are talking about. If I were in your place, I would look about for some tall, slim, black-eyed lady, farmer's daughter (contrast, you know). Be sure she has a good disposition, and then court her slowly and surely."

Mr. Scudder's countenance betrayed doubt, wonder, finally decision. He spoke firmly, with one eye on the door, expectant of Hester, "*You can have me yourself, Dorothy.*"

"I? Oh, I, Mr. Scudder! You could find a wife that would be a great deal better for you. I have the highest opinion of your moral worth; but it is just as I said, — we must keep together."

"You can come, every one of you! the farm is big enough,— old lady and all,— yes, every mortal fellow of you!" exclaimed Mr. Scudder, too excited to be elegant in language any longer.

Dorothy struggled with the fun of that last declaration and her real admiration for his generous nature.

"You are a large-souled man, Mr. Scudder, and I thank you with all my heart; but please don't give this idea another serious thought. We are all attached to the old homestead, and all so — so independent, you would not understand us, — no, not one of us!"

Mr. Scudder regarded Miss Dorothy mournfully; but he saw it was of no use to urge his suit. He looked at the photographs, then back at her, remarking in a depressed way, "Well, if it is no go, there is no use crying over it. Don't you say any thing about it, will you, Miss Prescott? Folks twit a widower so everlastingly about such things!"

"I will never mention it to a person," said Dorothy promptly. "I shall take an interest in you; and, if I can help you in any way, I certainly will at any time."

Mr. Scudder sat silently cogitating on that last remark of hers. It had a cheering influence. "Thank you, thank you for *that!* I have always heard you girls were smart. Anybody you would advise would be likely to be a little above par. I don't want to be taken in; and, as long as I have begun on this kind of thing, I might as well carry it through."

Dorothy thought of the beautiful farm, of the goodness of this simple man in the stiff shirt-collar and big seal-ring, of the many worthy women who wanted a home, and she resolved to help him to a wife. Her motive was benevolence and a wee bit of private fun. She gave him her hearty sympathy and promise of aid. Hester at this point returned, and packed the pictures very neatly for transportation. Mr. Scudder took them with expressions of approval, and prepared to go home. He shook hands with each lady, but said to Dorothy, as he was going out of the door, under his breath, "I will call in a week or so: meanwhile you think about " —

Dorothy's face was demure; but the riotous, pent-up fun made her whisper, "About *she as is to be*!"

Mr. Scudder nodded like an excited Chinese mandarin, and backed out hurriedly with "she as was" tucked carefully under his arm.

Not a word of that interview did Dorothy divulge; but for many a day the amusement her thoughts seemed to afford her was the occasion of remark in the family.

. . . .

Mr. Severn looked toward the Howells' mansion every day with much solicitude, which was purely apprehensive. When the guests went away, he would be expected to go back, and he was so comfortable where he was. Everybody let him alone here, and they were attentive to him across the road. Had he been conceited and lazy, the atmosphere of the Howells's home would have been refreshing; but he was a guileless, scholarly man, with a rugged strength of character hidden under a gentle, quiet manner. He discovered, after a few days, that at the Howells' the ladies were masquerading in a harmless but very tiresome way. He would in the morning, for instance, have preferred to drink his coffee while he found out from plain Jacob Howells something of the early history of the town; but Miss Maude always came down to the table with a burning desire to converse on Indo-European and Semitic relationships, or some similar topic. He was ready to give her the benefit of his knowledge, accounting it not much at the best; but, hers being infinitely less, the exercise was not to him exhilarating. Moreover, mother Howells was constantly administering little sops of flattery, and repeating the compliments bestowed upon him by his parishioners. He thought them all very kind, but he enjoyed it no more than living in a room hung with mirrors.

Here at the Prescotts' nothing was done for effect. Everybody was simply natural. When Granty talked with him he recognized, back of her little oddities, the well-educated gentlewoman. Dorothy's brisk and breezy personality interested him as much as Hester's classical face, and shy, cold manner. He never heard *her* speak of "art;" and yet, if a pencil found its way into her fingers, she was soon sketching somebody or something. She saw every curious plant or weed if she went for a walk; she decorated the house with rare combinations of the old-fashioned flowers from the garden. Everywhere about the various rooms were her studies of fruit, flowers, birds, bits of landscape, and even attempts at modelling. If he tried to discuss them, she was as communicative as a child unwillingly catechised. To let Hester alone, or, better still, to oppose her, was to see her in her most interesting light, as he had already fond out.

One morning after breakfast, Mr. Severn lingered in the dining-room, and, turning to Dorothy, said, "Miss Prescott, I believe it was intended that I should live on *this* side of the road. You remember I gravitated directly here in the first place, but you put me immediately out in the cold. Later you had to yield, not to me, but to circumstances. I want so much some plea for urging you to keep me now you have me. How can I conciliate you? I will study the newest theories as to cows and hens, or any of these matters you have so much sport over. I will go to market for Miss O'Flarity. I will get Jack through the multiplication-table when he gets back. All this and much more will I do, if you will not thrust me out again. — Can you not plead for me, Mrs. Pepperfield?" he asked, turning to aunt Huldah, who sat in a cosey corner, with pink roses in her pretty breakfast-cap.

"I feel a great deal safer," said she, " to know that there is a man in the house, and I should think the rest would."

"Very true. And I forgot to mention that I would lock that particular cellar-door I have heard spoken of: I will do it every night regularly," added Mr. Severn, laughing.

"Uncle Jack left us two revolvers," said Hester suggestively.

"And I would no more touch one than I would fly to the moon!" ejaculated Granty.

"In case of any trouble," said Hester coolly, "I should fire one, no matter where I hit."

"I am a good shot. If I took aim with the other, the fortress would be doubly secure," said he.

"What will the Howells think?" asked Granty.

"They were so very kind to me, I should not think of asking a dismissal, if I could not urge that they need my rooms in all cases of company. This house is larger and quieter. I can study much better here, for several reasons."

"Well, if that is so," returned Granty, "and you can arrange it with them, you are welcome to stay."

Mr. Severn went away with pleased alacrity, determined to settle the matter that very day. It was going to be a blessed thing, he assured himself, to abide with these sincere people. Hester, he knew, had not said, "Come," because she was not sure that she wanted him; but he would not make himself disagreeable. If Granty wished him chiefly as a burglar-alarm, never mind; that was much better, he secretly reflected, than to have Miss Maude mark him for her own as a listener to her ideas on Sanscrit literature. He told the Prescotts at dinner-time that it was all pleasantly arranged with Mrs. Howells; and by night his books, trunks, and himself were permanently settled under their roof. To keep a minister who would insist upon staying was not the same plebeian thing as taking a common boarder, in Granty's aristocratic opinion. She was well pleased that he had become one of the family.

That same afternoon Hester was training a woodbine to grow over an apple-tree stump in the yard, when Molly Howells came across the street, and joined her. Hester liked Molly very much: there was a hearty truthfulness about her that made her often shocking to her sisters, but was not disagreeable to others. She was a tall girl, with strong limbs, large, well-defined features, and a voice a trifle loud; but this was because of strong lungs and hearty physique, not from a bold or coarse nature."

"You have Mr. Severn over here now," she exclaimed, seating herself in a rustic chair. "I am glad of it! I like him; but it was a bore to have him at our house, for *me;* and I am not sure it would not have been for the rest, after a while. We all had to take a European trip again the first thing."

"What do you mean?" asked Hester.

"Why, you know we went abroad five or six years ago. All I remember is a jumble of churches, pictures, parks, waiters, beer, no gas, no bath-tub, half the time, nothing much I liked to eat, and mamma worrying over our trunks all the time. But, since Mr. Severn came, we have been studying our guide-books to see where we went, and what we must have seen, so as to be able to talk about it. We were only gone three months, and of course we have forgotten —I have—all the pictures and statuary anyway. Maude declares she has not. Oh, I wish I had something to do I enjoyed! I wish I had a whole dozen little brothers and sisters to dress and teach and scold and play with. I can't be intellectual if I try; and I just told mamma to-day I will not drag through books I hate and do not understand, if they are *standard*. You are so smart over here, you think I am dreadful, probably. Oh, dear!" and Molly heaved a strong sigh from her robust chest.

"What is the matter, Molly?" asked Dorothy, appearing with a coil of wire for Hester's vine.

"I would like to get married," said Molly very deliberately after a moment. And then, at the peal of laughter that greeted her confession, she explained, in the most matter-of-fact way, "I never thought of it before until to-day. You see, if I had a kind of a shiftless husband, and ever so many children, and not too much money, I could sew and cook and wash and rush things, because it would be my *duty*. I hate puttering around a house full of servants, and being so genteel: I feel like a fool!"

Molly gave her coarse black hair a toss, and writhed in her chair until it creaked with her weight. Dorothy gave her a long, searching look. Hester knew by intuition what ailed the girl. The Howells came of a strong, hard-working stock on the father's side. In Molly had returned the body and mind of some aunt or grandmother who had been a good-hearted, sensible housewife, — a spinner, churner, bread-maker, a stirring, conscientious mother of vigorous children. Molly's mother did not understand that out of such material she could no more make a girl full of airs, graces, arts, accomplishments, and coquetry, than one could turn a pound of sweet country butter into a frothy Charlotte Russe.

Dorothy studied Molly during all the rest of the interview with a certain new interest. At last she exclaimed with vivacity, "Will you take a ride with me, Molly, to-morrow afternoon?"

"I should be delighted to do so," she answered.

"Very well: I will call for you about four o'clock. I am going to the swamp for some ferns, and have two or three errands besides."

Soon Molly remembered that her mother wished her to go shopping for her, and went away yawning. She had not made a fruitless visit, however: she had suggested several ideas to Miss Dorothy, and Dorothy's ideas were busy little workers.

CHAPTER XII.

"One of Marion's Sort."

IT was one of these rainy days that people call "old-fashioned," as if modern weather were light and trifling in kind. Uncle Pepperfield had business in the city which Marion begged him to delay, but he could not. All day the rain poured against the windows, blotting out the landscape, beating on the panes as if enraged at the cheer and comfort within. Jack made telephones and fire-engines, boiled molasses candy, and rehearsed to the black cook a medley of "Rip Van Winkle," "Robinson Crusoe," and "The Last of the Mohicans." In the afternoon it grew dark very early; and that, with the chill in the air, suggested to Dinah that aunt Pepperfield made a fire on such days. So she brought an armful of wood, and soon had a great blaze in the dining-room grate, with which to greet Mr. Pepperfield on his return. The brightness drew Marion from her book, and Jack nestled down with her in the soft rug on the hearth. She was building a rather lofty castle on the top of a particularly rosy flame, when in came Dinah again with a large envelope and a "Spec dis here is fur you: one of de neighbors fotched it as he was gwine along home." Marion, seeing in the corner the printed words, "Office of 'The Phœnix,'" tore it open a little more eagerly than usual, and read these lines in a singularly black and ugly handwriting:—

Miss Marion Prescott.

Dear Madam,—Your article has been read and approved. We accept it with thanks. Payment on publication.

Respectfully,

W. Craig.

"Very good, very good, brother Craig!" said Marion; while Jack looked up to see whom she was addressing so fraternally, but did not find out. Soon Dinah came back again, this time to set the table; for Mr. Pepperfield would be, she declared, "hungry as a bar," after walking up hill from the station in the wind and rain. Her task done, and the firelight dancing gayly over the silver and china, she retired to fill the air with the aroma of coffee. Soon, loud above the tumult of the storm, arose a shrill screech from the approaching engine.

"There comes uncle Pepper!" cried Jack, as if the old gentleman was entirely responsible for the signal.

He gave the fire a poke, and hopped off the rug to watch Marion go and fill a vase with scarlet geraniums, and put it on the table, remarking, the while, that it was just the color of the pretty sack she had put on for comfort.

Ten minutes later she heard a step, and hurried forward to open the outer door. Uncle Pepperfield it was, dripping like a fountain, and behind him another umbrella, held much higher, under it, as she discovered, another man, who was hospitably pushed in, and introduced.

"Look at that, now, Craig!" exclaimed Mr. Pepperfield, catching sight of the blazing fire. "Did I not tell you you would find something better here than away over the hill in your bachelor's boarding-house?"

"Did I say I doubted it, Mr. Pepperfield?"

"*Why*, if it isn't *you!*" cried Jack, ceasing to embrace the ancient cat, and presenting himself before Mr. Craig with a radiant visage. "Don't you remember me and aunt Marion? And are you always on the cars when it rains?"

"I had forgotten you until this moment," said Mr. Craig; "but I will make amends for it, my boy."

From Jack his glance returned to the lady playing hostess in Madame Pepperfield's place; and he was certainly aware that he had seen her before, and that not alone in the cars. Mr. Pepperfield saw his perplexity, and exclaimed, "Yes: you have seen her before. She called on you, but you did not ask her to stay to tea. Now, when you return her article, if you say any thing saucy about it, I will shoot you. She is under my protection."

"I accepted Miss Prescott's article yesterday; and I wondered greatly where in Ingleside there was a lady capable of writing it. I did not suppose I should follow my letter, or, it may be, precede it."

"No: I have it already," said Marion, trying to stop Mr. Pepperfield, who shamelessly continued, "You might have known her several weeks ago; but, when I proposed asking you to tea, she said she had no great opinion of literary people, and would not be one herself if she could help it. Editors in particular she regarded as necessary evils, to be endured, not encouraged, and "—

"Don't you pay the least attention to his falsehoods, Miss Prescott," said the guest, taking an easy-chair by the fire. "Since his last defeat at chess, he has tried every way to injure me. He would not have asked me here to-night, if Mrs. Pepperfield had not told him he must once in so often."

Dinah appeared, beaming over a platter of fried oysters; and the cold and hungry gentlemen were not averse to satisfying their sharpened appetites.

The conversation ran on cheerily. Mr. Craig had recently returned from a trip to California; and they talked of the West, until Jack unexpectedly put forth a conundrum fearfully made; when the editor of "The Phœnix" supplied him with a worse one for some other occasion. After supper Marion brought out the chess-board, that they might not feel bound to entertain her, and the game began.

Mr. Pepperfield was a player who took quarter-hours between his moves for deliberation,— intervals that Mr. Craig improved by talking with Marion. At first they spoke only of general matters; but, after a while, Marion found herself telling quite fully of her work, of what she had written, and why she had not written otherwise than she had.

"I liked your article," said Mr. Craig, "because I saw it had not been easily written in some library, with a note-book and pencil. There is a class of would-be essayists who must be bankrupt in an hour, if books were banks, and could close when there was too great a run on them. I know more than one individual who flourishes, like the pot of green basil, on somebody's else brains."

"What is the use of wearing out your own head in trying to be original," argued Mr. Pepperfield, "if you can use some other fellow's, and the public in general not know the difference? When I write for the press, I shall keep a 'common-place' book, as they used to call them."

"And it may be we shall call your articles by the same title," laughed Mr. Craig.

"Uncle Pepperfield!" broke in Jack, who found the conversation stupid, "you must come out to the grove to-morrow, and see our aquarium. I have got about a dozen Pilgrim Progress folks paddling around in it. Apollyon is the biggest old bull-frog you ever heard croak; and there is Great Heart and Christina, and the boy that ate Beelzebub's apples, and Mr. Brisk, who was Mercy's beau you know — or he wanted to be. He is a tadpole, and she is the cutest little green toad."

"What a moral and instructive exhibition it must be, Jack!" said Mr. Craig. "Can I be allowed to see it when I have a holiday?"

"Yes, you can, sir," continued Jack, determined to keep the floor, now he had it. "Once I had one at home, three mud-turtles in a pail in the back-yard; but, when they were in the water, Granty said they gasped for air, and must be tired swimming around and around: if I took them out, she said they looked all parched up, and pawed out in misery. I just went and heaved them into the creek, where I wouldn't be bothered to tell if they were happy or not. — O uncle!" he cried, getting more excited,

"Hester says she is going to have hens and roosters soon. Then won't we have a nice lot of animals!— Old Mortality, Buttercup, and the big dog. Dorothy hates hens. Uncle Jack used to hate them too: he said they were spluttering, tedious old fusses."

There was nothing in Jack's chatter to interest a stranger; but, listening to it, Mr. Craig found himself bewildered to know where he had heard something like it before. Hester, Granty, uncle Jack! He knew no such persons; yet he had heard their names, and that recently. Was it only that day with Jack on the cars? He let Mr. Pepperfield get the advantage of him in chess. He forgot to talk until he remembered the letter and the photograph. He looked keenly then at the little lady, whose fingers were moving quickly through a heap of snowy wool, and he was as sure that he had her picture in his keeping as he was puzzled to know how he came by it in the first place.

He leaned back in his chair, while uncle Pepperfield gloated over his prospective victory. He finally said, "Miss Prescott, I must have met you here in previous years: your face is not quite that of a stranger; or perhaps I have seen a picture of you here, and grown familiar with that."

"No," said uncle Pepperfield. "We have not a picture of one of you girls. Hester promised me one of hers."

"I sent aunt Pepperfield one of myself last spring. Perhaps you have seen that, Mr. Craig. I do not think I ever saw you before I came to Ingleside this time."

"Huldah never showed me any picture," persisted Mr. Pepperfield. "I do not believe we ever received it, or it would certainly have been on the wall in a fancy frame of some sort. She delights in such things."

"Oh, I sent it, uncle! for I remember what a long, long letter, all of family doings, went with it," responded Marion. To which Mr. Pepperfield made answer thus, "Well, perhaps it is among the 'articles of virtue and bigotry' at the dead-letter office."

Mr. Craig applied himself to the chess-board with a smile that caused uncle Pepperfield to twit him of trying to "grin and bear it," *it* being the probable loss of the game. When he had lost it beyond dispute, he returned to Marion, saying, "You have never sent any article before this to 'The Phœnix'?"

"No, I have not. Several months ago I wrote one for it; but after it was ready, even to the address, I decided it was not suitable. You had a narrow escape, you see."

Uncle Pepperfield pushed aside the chess-board, and took Jack on his knee. As the evening advanced, he was pleased to remark the variety of topics discussed by these two "literary characters," as he persisted in calling them. When the conversation was most animated, he settled back in a sleepy-hollow chair, and closed his eyes in meditation. Two hours later, a gentle snore brought Mr. Craig to his feet, and uncle Pepperfield back to consciousness. Jack was found to be fast asleep in the hearth-rug; and good-nights were in order. Mr. Craig forgave Mr. Pepperfield for glorying in his victory, expressed his pleasure at meeting Miss Prescott, and went home.

"Good fellow that, as ever lived," said Mr. Pepperfield, locking the door behind him. "I'm glad I met him on the train to-night."

. . . .

The next day Marion had a letter from Granty, which ran thus:—

MY DEAR CHILD,— I suppose you think it strange that I have not taken time to write you; but you know how full my hands always are. I often wonder what will become of you all when I am laid aside. Your uncle Jack used to say that the Lord always provided for the lame and the lazy, and as a family I do think we have great reason to praise him. I presume Hester told you of the tea-party. On my own account, I should not have thought of such an undertaking; but your aunt Pepper is fond of society, and, if you girls would have friends, you must show yourselves friendly. We all enjoyed it; Dorothy's cake and salads were excellent, and my raised biscuit were light as feathers. Mrs. Howells complimented them greatly, and well she might: hers are often heavy as lead when she has company. They have a house full of company over there now, from the West, and we have taken in Mr. Severn. Hester likes him very much: she says he hasn't any piosity, whatever she may mean by that. I was actually afraid she would not be civil to him, you know she is so queer sometimes; but yesterday she took him in the phaeton six or seven miles to see one of his sick parishioners. He was driving, and telling her about a day he spent in the ruins of Karnac. She had her parasol before her eyes to keep out the sun, and did not know he was absent-minded when interested in talking. The first thing Hester knew, he had driven right down a narrow lane, and brought the horse's nose blunt up against the back of a shed. They had to get out and unharness, and back out the horse and carriage, and altogether had a ridiculous time. Hester says it was like nothing but the doings of that absurd Peterkin family, in Jack's magazine. By the way, are you reading that serial in the "New Monthly"? It is a most miserable mess. The scene is laid in New England, about fifty years ago, and the writer does not know what she is trying to write about. I was just twenty years old at that time, and I assure you I saw such society as you never have seen, and probably never will see. This writer attempts to describe the etiquette of the first circles of Massachusetts and the old aristocracy of the time. O Marion! When I recollect the dinners at old Col. Winchester's (my mother's half-brother), and those at my aunt Atherton's,—the silver, the china, the wines, the venerable servants as stately as their masters and mistresses,—I realize what has passed away forever. Such a namby-pamby description as this one I speak of makes me indignant. If I had time and practice, I would try something of the sort myself. Only to tell of the balls I have attended! the dresses and jewels I have seen! There is nothing imported like them nowadays, I am sure. The Howells were very much dressed at our tea-party. Blanche had a very uncouth-looking blue silk thing on, although Dorothy says it was very stylish. I suppose I am behind the times. It is really deplorable to be wrapped up in the world and the things that perish with the using. Now, Marion, I have done something that I fear you will not like. Hester censured me quite severely; but I had no idea of doing any thing out of the way. There came along a distressed creature, with a printed paper, saying she had nine children scattered along between here and Albany, where she wanted to get to friends. Her husband was sick, and, dear me! I can't tell her troubles! I looked for something to give her, and came across that drab poplin of yours. I thought you must have got a good deal of wear out of it, and would not mind: so I let her have it. Hester says you had not worn it much. If this is true, I am sorry; but it cannot be helped. You know the Bible says, "He that giveth to the poor lendeth to the Lord." I do wish such creatures would not come along, and put me in such positions. There is that rag-and-tin man! I gave him, six weeks ago, two suits of your uncle's clothes out of the garret, and he has only brought me one small tin dipper. How can people be so unprincipled? It makes me sick of living sometimes. Dorothy paid the fire-insurance yesterday. It seems a great waste of money; for we never get any return for it: we may some day, however. It is hard to conduct this great house economically. I do my best, and often reason with your sisters. They make many expenditures *I* do not think judicious, like this never-ending tax-paying. I tell them I would have nothing whatever to do with it any more. Mrs. Howells is making a beautiful hearth-rug of a new kind of wool and silk floss. She bought the pattern, materials, and a book of directions, at Colburn's, near Fourteenth Street. You might just inquire how they sell them, when you are in the city some time. I do not get out much, and I like some little work of this sort when I am too tired to read. Take good care of yourself and of Jack. Don't let him get lost, if you take him into the city. We miss you, but hope you are having a pleasant time.

Your affectionate aunt.

"O Granty, Granty!" cried Marion, "my pretty poplin with the silk vest, and buttons that cost one dollar a dozen, and now 'scattered between there and Albany'! And Hester goes philandering down a lane that has no turning, and never considers how she is to get out. Ominous lane! Talking about the ruins of Karnac! I wish he had spent all his days there instead of one. I wish aunt Pepperfield would come home! I am tempted to crack a china cup, and tell her Dinah did it, and that she acts as if she had started on a mad career of more cracks. I will write Hester myself: perhaps she needs to hear from me."

"Aunt Marion, come down stairs! uncle Pepperfield wants you to see his day lilies," cried Jack. And Marion went.

CHAPTER XIII.

Part of a Letter from Marion to Hester.

.   .   .   .

"I THINK Mr. Severn must be a harmless sort of a person, although I shall be sorry to find him settled under our vine and fig-tree when I get home. Tell Dorothy not to let him fall a victim to her seductive good-nature. I neither wish him troubled by a fruitless passion, nor do I wish Dorothy sacrificed. How can a woman be deluded enough to marry a minister, no matter how good he is! If he is puffed up by conceit and spiritual arrogance, as many of them are — What does she do? She herself must marry the parish, no matter what is said to the contrary; and then, if she is faulty, she will be shot through and through like St. Sebastian. If she is lovely, she will realize, just the same, that she has no continuing city here this side of paradise. Think of having no permanent home, of always planting flowers for the next-comer to pick, of having every little while to box up what Mrs. Partington calls your 'liars and peanuts,' and be like poor Jo, forever moving on, to unpack them all broken, to have your carpets misfitted through all time, to be snubbed and patronized, and insulted with donation-parties! Then there is something worse than all the rest. How terribly bored an intelligent woman would be, after a while, by having always to listen to her own husband's sermons! It is impossible not to know the intellectual limitations of most mortals with whom we live long. We may never get to the end of their goodness, be often surprised by their heroism; but we do find out just about what they will say, think, and write, under every ordinary circumstance. It would not be of the least consequence if one's husband were a companion merely; but as a *teacher*, always teaching you in sentences that from previous associations you could finish for him, if he choked midway; preaching after a fashion you know, as one knows a wall-paper at which one has gazed for years — the idea is dreadful! Dorothy could not endure it. But I forgot that I was not writing an essay on ministers' wives — poor wretches!

"Tell aunt Huldah that Mr. Craig comes very often to play chess with uncle Pepperfield. She will tell you about him. I congratulate myself upon having made his acquaintance. He teaches me much, that, if I had known before, would have been of great value to me in my literary work. I mean not so much in regard to what or how to write as to matters of understanding among editors and journalists. Then he is a sharp critic: a beggarly thought in a fine coat gets sent flying the moment he espies it. My characters have to prove their reasons for being, for doing, and for suffering. If they are stuffed with sawdust, they collapse; if they are crude in aim, or lacking in finish, if I have narrated events where I should have cast a scene, I am told of it all with great clearness. Moreover, Mr. Craig is very companionable, and seems a big-brother sort of man, roguish and warm-hearted, so that Jack adores him" . . .

Hester received this letter one morning in the barn, whither she had gone to see if Pete had given the cow pumpkins cut in pieces suited for mastication. He had been to the post-office, and taken out this letter, which she began to read carelessly. "Dorothy a minister's wife! She must be wild! — Pete, don't you twitch Buttercup's head. A cow should be treated very gently: they don't like rough handling.

"*Mr. Craig* again! She writes about him in each letter. 'Comes often to play chess, — very companionable!'"

Hester suddenly sent a peck-measure spinning from her toe, half across the barn, toward Pete, who was looking for it, and said sharply, "Nail up that hole under the meal-bin, or the rats will get into the meal."

Out of the envelope fell a note, unseen before. It was unmistakably in Jack's hieroglyphics.

DEAR ANT HESTER, — It is jolly here. Dinah is awful fat, and shiny black. She makes me tarts every single day. Ant Marion wishes she would not, because I have the stomach-ache sometimes: that's nothin'; for Granty says children always have growing-pains. If anybody comes this way, please send me a roll of brass wire I left, and a box of awl sized nails, portickelarly *brads;* also My Pig-Sticker sled, in case it snows before I return. Mr. Craig comes to see Ant Marion most as often as Bridget O'Flarity's cousin comes to our house; but his hair is not red. It is a stationary thing for him to come evenings. Dinah wares a Big Green ring, her wedding one. I asked her where her Husband was, and she said she "specked he was a-plowin' the red-hot furrows of hell." Ant Marion was Shocked. She said it was dreadful to say; and Dinah, she said, "What's de use a-curtailin' de troof." If it is wicket to repeat this, you had better skip it. Mr. Craig is a writin'-fellow too, like Ant Marion. I wish they'd write a newspaper together, and let me screech it around like the New-York Boys. She could make the stories, and he put in the dry stuff. He says maybe he would. I must go to bed. Good-night, and pleasant dreams.

JACK PRESCOTT.

P.S. — Hens have the pip and the yawns — no gapes — I have heard since I got here. You better study about these in the medical books. If we keep 'em, we don't want sick hens a-sprawling around our handsome coop, if we ever have one. Also. If You should Shave old mortality's Hair close to his Skin, he will be mouse-color; and this is Stylish for horses. I will ask if it is done with a Razor. I do pray for myself now. Ant Marion puts me in mind of it, and for all the rest of you. I send my best love to Granty. JACK.

Jack's letter only deepened the cloud on Hester's countenance. She thrust it into her pocket, and went about the barn, finding out Pete's delinquencies, and visiting them on his head like Nemesis herself. She returned to the house, and wasted no words for the rest of the day.

"What is the matter with you?" asked Dorothy at night. Hester had entered the latter's bedroom, and was leaning grimly over the foot of her couch.

"Marion will make a fool of herself," she answered.

"What do you mean?"

"Why, she will just get infatuated with that editor. Aunt Huldah says he is handsome and cultured, and so on. I do not like it at all. I wish she had never gone to Ingleside. Here we three are, old enough to be done with such nonsense. I don't wish to get married; you don't: why should she. We can be so perfectly independent here by ourselves, — no one to order, interfere, or to criticise us; but let her bring a *man* in, and think of it! We all must revolve around him like satellites. He says this, or he likes that and the other."

"Nonsense!" said Dorothy: "you are a goose yourself. Do you suppose the editor of the largest journal of its sort in the country is going to bury himself in a little village, for the sake of domineering over one old lady and two poor creatures like you and me?"

"Well, then it is all the worse: Marion will leave us. They, being two blue lights, will become one, and he will be it. She never will write that book that is to make the family glorious: she will settle down to mending his gloves, and quoting his opinions. If she wanted to marry, why didn't she take that rich young Sprague years ago?"

"He was not half baked, Hester: he was a regular dough-head."

"I know. But he only lived six months, though, to be sure, she could not have relied upon that beforehand," returned Hester, with such solemn animosity, that Dorothy was moved to inquire if Mr. Craig had said any thing of significance matrimonially to Marion.

Hester gravely wagged her head, and went on like a judge charging a jury. "You see, Marion may have been turning soft this long time, and we not realize it. She has written many stories: they had to be more or less *love* stories, or the public was not suited: so a gradual demoralization has been going on in her, perhaps"—

"Do you think it demoralizing to fall in love?" asked Dorothy meekly.

"Certainly. Her principles being in this way undermined, she goes to Ingleside, meets this remarkable man of similar tastes, and anybody can foresee the result."

"Marion is young yet," returned Dorothy reflectively,—"young and very good-looking, intellectual, and nice. I do not know why she should not marry. I never settled it that she should not."

"I had," said Hester firmly.

"And for *me?*"

"Certainly."

"Well, I am obliged to you," returned Dorothy

frankly; "but if a good, agreeable man, with some money, ever wants me, and I want him, I shall do as I please."

The surprise on Hester's face was really unfeigned; and, to Dorothy's pointed question that followed, she gave also a direct answer.

"To be sure," said Dorothy, "we are not young girls any longer; we have no property, nor much beauty, and we shall probably never be led into temptation: but don't you ever think of a *possibility?*"

"A possibility?" echoed Hester, with a toss of her head very fine in its way. "With such actualities as having to find Old Mortality in horse-feed, oats at the price they are now; or experimenting on that Jersey cow, to know what food is best for milk; with bearing on my mind the potato-barrel, the locking of the doors at night, the mixing complexions for all the faces I've had to paint lately; and the administering cough-drops and yellow mixture to uncle Jack's old patients; trying to make myself happy, moreover, in the belief that we shall always live on the fat of the land, because Granty came from Massachusetts, — with · all this, Dorothy Prescott, what time do you suppose I find to muse, like Agamemnon, 'on things that never are to be'?"

Dorothy was impressed; but she ventured to ask how she knew that Agamemnon ever did it.

"Well, if you must know, I read it in Mr. Severn's translated 'Iliad,' in the office, which is already half-full of his books. Oh! I tell you, Dorothy, the Philistines are upon us from more directions than one."

"Never mind; go to bed," returned her sister. "I am sleepy; and I do not believe but that Marion can take care of herself. I never saw a Prescott who could not."

Hester went, muttering ominously.

CHAPTER XIV.

An October Day.

MR. CRAIG was driving slowly up the hill at Ingleside, going toward Mr. Pepperfield's. This fact was easily explained by another: he was going to ask Miss Prescott to take a ride with him. For a quiet bachelor, Mr. Craig had become quite gallant of late: several people had remarked upon it — but not to him. He himself began to be conscious that his editorial mind was exercised often with other matter than that which ran in his usual line of thought. Perhaps "exercised" is too violent a word: *occupied* might be better. When he came at night from the city, it was so easy to stop for a chat with Mr. Pepperfield at the gate: it was easier yet to go in for a game, and a talk with Marion. The more he saw of her, the more her grace and excellence pleased him; then she had a high order of talent, and was not conceited. He was thinking this as he rode up the hill, and was regretting that her visit was drawing near its end. He had never told her that he had her picture, or thought it advisable to return the letter. Yes: he should be lonely after she had gone. She gave zest to chess: she was a more interesting talker than aunt Huldah, and a more inspiring listener. Feminine companionship and sympathy were good for a man.

The scholarly editor of "The Phœnix" evolved this truism from his inner consciousness with the earnestness of one who unearths something valuable seldom brought to light. He had not a thought that every Paddy he passed on the road had thus reflected before he found his Peggy.

Not that Mr. Craig was sentimental with any malice aforethought on this occasion. He had not a fleeting thought to ask Marion not to go home, or ever to come back: he only wished that she would not cease to be where he could find her when he wanted society.

He arrived at Mr. Pepperfield's in due time, and had only to wait a moment before Marion appeared. She looked so trim and rosy, in a dark, quaint little hat with a bright vine about it, that he wished she had been a sister or cousin, or somebody whom he might salute in a more cordial way than by a touch of his kid glove to hers.

"Where shall we go?" he asked, as they were seated in the carriage.

Marion answered promptly, "Let us see as much of the woods as possible."

No one would have questioned her taste. It was the first day of October, and the afternoon was wonderful. There was not the usual haze of autumn in the air; but the sun poured down light as intensely as in June. The fields of winter-wheat showed under it the brightest green that nature ever gives. Edging these fields were hedges of sumach: every tiny leaf thereon was a flame of scarlet or yellow; and the whole showed against the background of pine-trees, like long wreaths and heaped-up garlands of the gayest flowers. In the sparser woods the foliage of the tallest trees was here and there unchanged in green, but thinned out; so that, from their roots to their topmost boughs, the red woodbine could be seen, intwining them in exquisite contrast of color. Along the roadside the wealth of beauty was bewildering. The golden-rod and purple asters nodded and danced together in the sunshine, as far as one could see, along every fence, lane, and boundary line. Every thing that had been coarse or ungainly through the immature spring and summer had come into a sudden estate of grace and beauty. The bursting milkweed-pods were shedding silvery, silky treasures: even the mullein-leaves had turned golden under the touch of a frost finger; and in or over every broken stone wall crept pretty vines that waved their little red banners as if they knew it was a brief holiday. Where the creek had sunken through the moss, in the low lands, the tall cat-tails and lush flags flourished; while the willow-trees near them were scattering pale-yellow leaves broadcast, and leaving their own soft outlines pencilled against the heavenly blue of the sky.

Bird-song could still be heard, though convocations of the songsters in certain trees showed what they were planning. Butterflies clustered on the thistle-blossoms; the bees were so noisy in the late clover and the buckwheat, that one forgot the great army of insects which had certainly vanished.

The two enthusiastic admirers of all this loveliness were not talking much as they rode. Neither of them was ever prodigal with adjectives; and, as friends, they were sufficiently at ease to be silent if they chose. They frequently stopped; and Mr. Craig stepped out of the carriage for ferns or flowers, in tempting looking places where the road ran through the swamp. At one point there was a rude settlement in a pine-wood: there the sumach-bushes were so gorgeous that Marion possessed herself of a branch, which glowed in her hand like fire. She was admiring it, when a child ran out from a cabin, and warned her that it was the poisonous kind, and might make her sick. She thanked him, and hid it until he vanished, explaining to Mr. Craig that she had handled it probably many times before with no ill effects.

"We have beautiful woods near our home," she continued, "but no hills."

"I would like to see your home and your family. It seems to me I must have known your uncle, you have made him so real a person to me," he returned.

"Yes: we would like to see you there. Dorothy you would understand at once, and like; Hester you would make nothing of."

Mr. Craig did not answer. He was wishing that Marion would write to him, thinking he would like to write to her, turning it over in his own mind like this: "If I ask her to correspond with me, does it mean that I have a peculiar interest in her? Have I — if I have, what then? What should we write of? I would wish her to write such comical familiar letters as *that one* to aunt Pepperfield. Absurd! I am not her aunt, and she is not going to treat me like one. I have it! I will not say any thing. I will write her from my office a business letter, of course, but modified, amplified, on account of ex-official friendship. When she answers, I will find matter for another and another and another. If she does not like this elasticity of business relations, she will show it by her coolness. If she does "— Marion broke in with a very matter-of-fact remark that called for a similar answer. He gave it, as well considered, apparently, as if he were not repeating to himself, "If she *does*," and thinking how soft her hair must be to the touch, there where it waved back from her temples, with the October light tangled into its curls and loops. Soon after, with the consistency of many another man in his situation, — one who has but just resolved *not* to do a certain thing, — he said, " I hope, Miss Prescott, you will often send us some article for 'The Phœnix.' If you will allow me, I can sometimes write you when a subject would be timely, giving you a hint how to work it up acceptably. You, perhaps, will give me occasionally some idea of what you are doing; and any help I can give you, you must rely on ; will you not?"

Marion thanked him cordially; and again they drifted into impersonal conversation. All the afternoon they rode by cosey farms, where, under the low-boughed trees in the orchards, the men were barrelling the heaped-up apples, and children were strolling down the lanes after beechnuts. When at last they turned, it was to go toward a sunset glorious with colors, which the very clouds seemed to have borrowed for once from the earth beneath. Before they faded, the moon rode up in the opposite heavens; and between the two radiances the world was at its fairest.

"This has been the most perfect day I have ever seem," said Marion.

"If you go home Thursday, I suppose this will be your last drive with me," said her companion slowly.

She replied, not at all dolorously, that it would be.

When they were once more home, Mr. Craig refused Mr. Pepperfield's invitation to remain to tea, on account of neglected writing to be attended to that evening. He then drove down the hill, wondering that he had not staid, puzzled over a certain melancholy that seemed about to tinge his usually cheerful views of life. He did not regret any thing that afternoon done. He was not actually sorry for those things he had left undone. His vague impression took form at last in the reflection, —

"Some men, in my place, would see a wife in that lady left behind me. No one need wait for a better one."

The editor of "The Phœnix" pensively asked himself if he were like other men, and, if not, why not.

He found a cigar in his pocket, lighted it, and laughed outright: nevertheless he imparted to his fleet horse this secret, "If she had offered herself to me this afternoon (that being the proper order of things), I should have said *Yes*."

CHAPTER XV.

What Came of Marion's Ride.

HESTER was idling in the hall one day, talking with aunt Huldah, who was knitting long red stockings for Jack, when Mr. Severn appeared at what was an unusual hour for him. She could not see that he had any reason for coming; and she felt like reproving him for the sin of idleness, which she herself was committing. Aunt Huldah was talking briskly, when Hester, happening to glance up, received a significant look from Mr. Severn, with a gesture which said, "Come, I wish to speak to you;" then he walked across the hall, out on to the piazza.

Hester, knowing he must mean her to meet him unobserved, went soon into the next room, and by another way reached the place where he was. He gave her at once a letter, saying, "This came in an envelope directed to me, but marked within for you: doubtless it will explain itself."

Hester, much surprised, hastily opened, and found it to be a note from Jack.

Dear Ant Hester,— Uncle Pepper has gone away for three days on buzinis, and Ant Marion is awful sick. She don't want to scare Granty, so she sed I could write you a note, and enclose it to Mr. Severn. He would give it to you when nobody was about. If Pete fetched it to any of the rest, she would see it. She don't know what ails her, and Dinah don't, either. She don't want a strange doctor fussing over her: so won't you come visiting, and take care of her? Explain to Dorothy and Ant Huldah. Dinah says it looks like errysipplous. Ant Marion says tifoid fever; but I bet smal pocks, 'cause she is spotted with big red spotts all over her hands and arms. She feels awful mean and headaky. Perhaps she'll die. I feel lonesome. I read the Bible, where Ant Pepper's best bookmark is, on the parlor table. Granty says it consouls her to read Chapters. This did not me. It sounded like swearing. It was all begats, begats, begats. What are they, anyway? Come as quick as you can, or she may be dead, and we having the funeral. Now she says it ain't no such thing, and she won't be dead. She hopes I have not alarmed you. I Have Not have I? She guesses it's Marmarial fever; but she would like to see you here. Her head akes so she can't correck This.
     Your Dear Jack.

Hester was alarmed, but sincerely hoped that Jack had expressed himself too strongly. She rapidly explained the letter to Mr. Severn, who had gone to the other end of the piazza, and was reading a newspaper. She told him that she should probably take the evening train for Ingleside, and then went back to find aunt Huldah and Dorothy. When they understood her, they made every thing easy by agreeing not to needlessly frighten Granty until they were sure Marion was dangerously ill. They would propose that Hester should go on and keep her there for a longer visit. The weather was so fine, Hester would enjoy the change, and have a chance to visit picture-galleries to her heart's content. There never was a more guileless soul to deal with than Granty. In half an hour she thought she had proposed the visit herself, and was sending more messages to Marion than Hester could remember, had memory been the one faculty she possessed.

That was a busy day. Hester went to her room: Dorothy followed, saying, "Now take clothes enough; because, if she is very sick, you may have to stay a long time, and, if she gets well right away, you might have a nice visit afterwards."

Hester replied, "Don't bother me with trifles. If Marion is sick, the question is, what ails her? Aunt Huldah says there is only one doctor in Ingleside, and he is just out of college. She must have the best medical advice; but I shall nurse her myself, if she does not die before I get there. See, here is the closet, there are my bureau-drawers. Tumble any thing you see fit into my trunk, only let me alone. I am going to the office to read about fevers and erysipelas. Do not call me for two hours at least."

Aunt Pepper appeared as Hester went; and she, with Dorothy, selected the articles they thought it best for Hester to take.

"I pity the doctor who has charge of any one that Hester takes care of. If he does not know just what he is about, she will see through him as soon as uncle Jack would," said Dorothy. "Ever since she could walk she has had a passion for inquiring into the diseases of his patients. As she grew older, it pleased him to take her to see curious cases, and to give her the newest works of medical writers to study. I think she could stand to-day as good an examination as most medical students could. Of course she never would put herself in the place of a physician, where there was responsibility, and he was the one to take it; but we would far sooner trust her than a doctor who was unknown to us. Oh, dear! I hope Marion is not going to be very sick."

"Oh, no! Being alone, she is frightened, and old Dinah has made her more so. Mr. Pepperfield will be back, even before Hester gets there: I am sure he will, from what he wrote me the first of the week," said aunt Huldah, rolling up stockings, and stuffing them into the trunk corners.

The ladies talked, worked, and secretly worried all the day; and at night Hester was off on the six-o'clock train, expecting to reach Ingleside early the next morning.

Now, leaving the family saddened by her departure, and fearful of the next news from Marion, we will follow Hester. She had no detentions, but arrived safely on time the day following. When the cars stopped, she stepped out on to the station-platform, and took a hasty look around, hoping to see some one sent for her. There were a few elegant private carriages waiting for some of her fellow-travellers, but none for her, and no hack or omnibus so far as she could discover. It was a lovely morning: the sun had been long up; but rosy clouds yet filled the sky, and the towers of the little village on the hill were softly outlined against the blue background; while winding in and out for a long way before her was the road overarched by the brilliant maple-trees. Hester was a good walker; but she had climbed that hill before, and knew how tantalizingly it stretched out and out, how tired one was when the top was gained. She was in haste to be with Marion; for who knew what had occurred since Jack's letter started? Go on wheels she must, if any were to be had for the purpose. So thinking, she espied a small, dark man, evidently a peddler, with his cart. It was clean; and she approached to state her case, hoping to engage his services. He was a well-behaved Hebrew, who could carry a conversation only so far as to tell her he was "Schultz der rags-beddler,

—*rags-beddler*," repeating it, with an evident desire to shout, in professional accents, "Ra–ags," but also restrained by a remnant of courtesy.

A broad-shouldered gentleman rushed around the corner of the station-house, and stopped with a quick glance at the two.

"I know you are a peddler; but, for half a dollar, can't you take me up the hill? I am in haste: I" — Suddenly she got out, in tolerably back-handed German, the same idea, with a rise to seventy-five cents, in good round English, at the end.

"Der rags-beddler" had no time to close in with the offer. The gentleman took her hand-bag, saying, "I have come for you, Miss Prescott: there is a carriage at the front of the platform now. Your sister is better. I ought to have been here before."

"Yes, certainly you had," said Hester, for the simple reason that it was the truth; and, as she turned promptly to follow him, Mr. Craig gave a glance at this brisk lady, whose dark hair was tossed roughly by the breeze, and whose clear-cut face was finer than Marion's, if it lacked the color and vivacity of expression hers had. He expected she would say it was no matter that he was late: Marion would have done so undoubtedly. She only followed, without a word, until they were in the carriage; then she said interrogatively, "You are Mr. Craig?"

"Yes. Your uncle did not return until late last evening. He telegraphed to the city for a doctor, who will be out in the next train."

"What doctor?"

"Dr. Willis Hilton, I believe."

Hester was silent a moment, then said, "He will do, perhaps. I should have preferred Dr. Gracie. Why did you not send for some one before? I think it wrong to have waited: there are diseases that can only be controlled if taken at the outset."

"What a fierce young woman!" thought the editor of "The Phœnix," who answered urbanely, "I have not seen Miss Marion since she was taken ill; but old Dinah told me she would have no one sent for until her uncle or you came. I could not take the liberty."

"You might. If Dinah thought her very sick, I think you ought to have done so," said Hester, with a vicious desire to quench this probable admirer of her sister, now a little anxiety was allayed.

Mr. Craig touched up his horses, and made no answer. He remembered that it had occurred to him, on his way to the station, that he might meet a nervous, tearful, elderly maiden, very grateful for his care, but requiring to be soothed by repeated assurances that her sister still lived. He felt, as it was, a little need of soothing himself. He had waited over a train this morning, for the sake of being of service to this pugnacious person, who was not tearful, nor nervous, nor apparently any older than her sister. Rolling along thus in silence, Hester may have had an intuition of his thoughts; for, without any prefix or addendum, she ejaculated, "I thank you for your trouble in coming for me. It was very kind."

"You need not. It was no trouble. I would do much more for your sister."

That was his one prick, so dexterously given that Hester almost forgave him.

She said nothing more, until she discovered that a shoe on one horse's foot was loose, and mentioned it as a fact having no interest for her, but something possibly well for him to know.

When they reached Mr. Pepperfield's, she thanked him again, and quickly disappeared in the house, before she knew, that, at Mr. Pepperfield's invitation, he intended to stay until the next train into the city; using the carriage to go to the station, and giving it to the doctor to come back with. Entering the house, he was welcomed by old Dinah, and soon after summoned by Mr. Pepperfield himself to breakfast. They were taking their second cup of coffee together when Hester re-appeared, taking her place at the table as if she and Mr. Craig had sat opposite one another their lives long. With more color, and less fierceness, she was decidedly pleasant to look upon, as that gentleman observed; while uncle Pepperfield asked, "Well, Hester, how do you find your patient? I am glad to see your face so much brighter than it was: it encourages me."

"I do not think she has any thing at all like typhoid-fever, or that she is very ill. It may be erysipelas; though I do not believe it is. I think she is more frightened at the eruption than at any thing else."

"I am delighted to hear it," said uncle Pepperfield: "we will cure her up soon. And, now that you have been plucked up and transplanted, you must take time, and flower out here in all your beauty, and — and — I would finish in style if I could."

"It is not the season of year to flower out," said Hester, taking a roll, and eating it meditatively. She broke into their discussion of political matters soon after, with the question, "Marion could not have poisoned herself, could she? She appears like a patient of uncle Jack's, who had been in the woods, and handled poisonous ivy."

"No," said Mr. Pepperfield. "She has" —

But he was interrupted.

"She has been to the woods, and she has handled poisonous sumach. I took her there, and she brought home her arms full," said Mr. Craig.

"Didn't you know any better?" asked Hester sternly.

"No, I did not," he answered meekly; adding courageously, in a minute, "Yes, we did know better. We were warned; but your sister said she did not fear its effects."

"You ought to have thrown it right away, whatever she said."

Mr. Craig was both amused and piqued by this remarkable sister, who persistently took high ground, and reproved him as if he were a child. He was accustomed to deference. He did not exact it; but he found he expected it, now that it was not forthcoming. She was not rude or unladylike: she was like fresh air suddenly turned on to one. It was natural to give way a little from the surprise of the thing, before knowing whether or not it was agreeable. The last cup of coffee finished, Mr. Craig found it time to start for the city, and bade them good-morning.

It was not long before Dr. Hilton arrived, and made a quick diagnosis. He confirmed Hester's suspicions, and laughingly declared that they had treated him shabbily in sending for another doctor, and drawing him into a consultation with one who was practising without a diploma. He professed to regret that he was to be played out of a long professional service; but he was sure Marion would recover in a day or two, with the proper remedies. Old Dinah rushed about to get a second hot breakfast for "that thar city swell-doctor, what do' no' no mo' nor Miss Hester did fust five minutes she war in de hous." And it was in vain Jack asked, "How could he, Dinah, if that was all there was to know?"

Marion herself smothered a good deal of laughter in her pillow, and grew rapidly better. She acknowledged that she had been greatly frightened, and chiefly at the great red spots on her hands: however, she did not regret sending for Hester.

"I will get well as quickly as possible, and we will take a few days to go about the city together; then I will go home, and you can stay a few weeks. But first unpack your trunk, and go to bed. Sleep until noon, and after that we will talk. If you travelled all night, you are tired."

Hester asserted that she was not sleepy, and her trunk had not been sent from the station: so after Mr. Pepperfield had taken away the doctor, and Dinah had made the invalid eat her breakfast, Marion, wrapped in a blanket, sat up among the pillows, and Hester settled herself in a big easy-chair.

"Now tell me all the news," said Marion. "How have you gotten along since I came away? You are not in debt, I hope."

"Not a penny! Trust Dorothy for that. No: aunt Huldah wanted to pay her board when she came, but we would not hear a word to it. She seemed to succumb; but she really has circumvented us, for she gets from Granty the state of our affairs, and orders and pays for all sorts of things. When we remonstrate, she says she is as much one of us as she ever was; and uncle Pepperfield told her to do such things, or he would be ashamed of her. Mr. Severn's board-bill, too, is not an insignificant item."

"What is he like?" asked Marion.

"He is not tediously pious in any outside-of-the-platter fashion; but he is good. The poor people in his church think there never was such a man; and the aristocratic ones are very fond of him, I hear. He talks with Granty about New England by the hour. When she says funny things, he laughs so heartily, I know nothing comical ever escapes him. We never find him in our way; and, best of all, he is not rooted and grounded in the idea that he knows every thing, as this Mr. Craig seems to be."

"Why, what have you seen of Mr. Craig?" asked Marion, opening wide her eyes.

"He brought me from the station; and there is altogether too much of him in some way."

"He can't help the breadth of his shoulders and the length of his limbs. I like him very much, and I thought you would. We see a great deal of him."

"So I thought, from your letters."

"How is Dorothy?" asked Marion, after a pause.

Hester's countenance relaxed; and she replied, laughing, "I used to think she had bewitched poor Mr. Scudder, he came so often, and staid so long. I half fancy that he offered himself, but I cannot find out. However, he still calls, and brings her fruit and flowers and unromantic vegetables. One day lately, Dorothy and Molly Howells went to ride. Dorothy had a basket, which she stopped to leave at the Scudders'. Mr. Scudder came out, and insisted that they should come in to see a new hothouse he was having made. Dorothy says he has a splendid farm, and the children are far more human than you would think from their photographs. Molly Howells was delighted with the dairy, and tried her hand at churning. She is such an honest, outspoken girl, the Scudder girls were greatly pleased with her; and Mr. Scudder, Dorothy said, seemed much impressed with her good-nature. On the way home she (Molly) said *he* was not so queer as she imagined him to be. Now, I believe Dorothy Prescott is *match-making!* She will not confess she is, but only says Molly is discontented at home, never will be stylish enough to suit her mother, and is pining for good sensible work."

"How funny!" exclaimed Marion. "What would her mother say?"

"Oh! if he were poor, she would banish Molly to Liberia before she would consent. But Mr. Scudder is very rich, and she will admit his good qualities undoubtedly, and tell people he is 'so eccentric.'"

At this point Hester's trunk arrived, and the conversation came to an end.

CHAPTER XVI.

Good Advice not Taken.

MARION'S room was quiet, and she was ready for work, so far as accessories were concerned. Her pens were new, her inkstand was refilled, the paper spread lavishly over her desk was clean and white. There was the trouble: she was not in a mood to make that paper a whit less white. It was an excellent day to sit down for hours of steady work. The rain was dashing against the window, and no caller would be likely to brave the December storm; but pens, ink, paper, and time never made a writer. Marion felt herself as dull as the dullest school-girl ever forced to write a composition. Her glance fell on a newspaper paragraph, where attention was called to "Miss Marion Prescott's last remarkably brilliant story in the December number of the ——, so 'unaffected in style,' of such 'power in portraying character,' so 'dramatic in plot, its conversations witty yet natural, the whole thoroughly exciting in a legitimate way,'" &c.

"How that reviewer flattered me!" she mused. "I never wrote such a story, or, if I ever did, I cannot any more."

She was staring at a great puddle in the road, and the many bubbles the raindrops made in it, when Dorothy, appearing behind her, cried, "Don't you waste a minute. Do you think, if I could coin my brains into money, I would stand gazing out of the window? I'm surprised at you."

Marion turned to the lively young woman, who wore a gingham apron with an account-book rising out of its side-pocket, then she said, "Dorothy, there are various ways of killing the goose that lays the golden eggs."

"Very likely. What is the latest way of doing it?" asked her sister, as she puffed a little with the exertion of running up stairs after her domestic labors.

"When uncle Jack was alive," said Marion, continuing the thoughts that occupied her when Dorothy came in, "I wrote because I delighted in it. I was continually seeing people who suggested to me other people, half made up of the peculiarities of these first, half formed out of my fancy. I made such characters to act in scenes suggested by other places, pictures, or, it might be, dreams. When I read, also, sentences would be texts to me for long trains of thought that would be worked out in me by a kind of happy spontaneity. In short, I never remember to have asked myself, ' *What* shall I write?' but only, 'Am I writing this that I have to write in the very best way?' When I read over the stories and sketches and essays of those times, they surprise me. There is so much in them, I feel, as you said one day about butter and eggs, 'How much must have been wasted in those days when we never thought any thing about it!' Now, the fact is, I have nothing to write about. I am used up."

Marion's manner was dejected; no doubt she spoke sincerely: but practical Dorothy could not understand it. She looked at the writing-desk, and then at the intellectual face of the young woman before it. Marion had not had softening of the brain, or any stroke of paralysis; and certainly the world was as full of queer characters as ever it was: why were they not just as suggestive?

"I did not suppose authors were like cisterns,— liable to get dry," she said.

"Well, they are."

"Then can't they be primed when they get out of order,— like old pumps?"

"I have tried priming. I read yesterday until my head ached: all I could think was, 'Oh that my enemy would write a book, and give me what he made by it!'"

"What do you suppose is the reason of this?"

"I have worked too hard and too fast. I have not let people and things quietly impress a 'mind at leisure from itself,' which is the secret of seeing things in a new light. I have felt the necessity of making capital for present work out of every available circumstance, and I feel dragged. I see nothing that interests me. If I had a fortune left me, I would not look at a pen for six months; then I could do better than ever before. I have learned much about the art of telling things; but what does that avail, if I have nothing to tell?"

"Well, it is unfortunate," said Dorothy. "The golden goose must have a rest, of course; but, as old Father Nelson used to inquire in prayer-meeting, 'How shall we best *preparate* for this vast future which is to come?' The coal-bin is half empty; the gas-bill is large; I can see the bottom of the flour-barrel, the sugar-barrel, and the soap-box. The money melts out of my pocket-book like snow off the roof."

"Do we live economically?" asked Marion.

"Yes; placed as we are, we do. There! the clock is striking eleven. I must go back and see about the dinner."

Left alone Marion gazed still more dolefully at the blank paper, murmuring, "If I had to sew, now, or to spin, I could say, '*You shall!*' to myself; but to be 'brilliant, effective, witty, dramatic, and thoroughly exciting in a legitimate way,' all under compulsion, only inspired by vanishing coal and soap and starch!" She was reflecting on the situation, when Jack appeared to show his rubber boots, with a hole in each where the heel ought to be; to modestly ask for a new overcoat; and also to make the general remark, that "a fellow liked new skates, when his old ones acted like flat-irons without any handles." It was a relief to Marion when the dinner-bell rang.

Dorothy was pre-occupied at the table; and Marion, as she ate, was wishing that Hester was home. Why, she could not have told; only Hester was always ready to propose either something practical in the way of action, or something so highly impractical, that it diverted them from melancholy into laughter. Mr. Severn and Granty had most of the conversation between them. He was not getting on rapidly in knowing Marion Prescott. She was usually the listener when others talked, and the one to disappear if he lingered long among them. He had read some of her articles, and liked them: she interested him all the more that she was so elusive.

"I wish that I had genius of the very grandest sort," said Dorothy suddenly, as she opened the coffee-pot, and looked in for some purpose; adding, as she shut it again,—"or a large fortune: I do not care which."

Everybody laughed at the outburst, but took no other notice of it. Mr. Severn reflected that it was the first time he had heard them speak of money. He thought them in quite independent circumstances. Their manner of living was simpler than the Howells's, but in better taste, and easier. To-day he reflected that this family might not be rich, but they could not be poor; for the young ladies were always elegantly dressed. Marion would have been amused to know that the deluded man based his opinion on the dainty bits of ribbon, velvet, and old lace, with which they brightened up their everyday dresses.

After dinner Marion turned her back on her writing-desk, and, entering the parlor, took a great chair by the open fire. Mr. Severn followed her, and spent most of the short, stormy afternoon talking with her. At first their conversation was impersonal; but, when Mr. Severn began to speak of her writings, Marion asked him if it ever happened to him, that, when he had a sermon to write, he found himself without any thing to say. Then, somewhat as she had to Dorothy, she told of her present inability to find people and things suggestive, as well as her difficulty in spinning fancies from internal resources. Of course she did not allude to the "flour-barrel," but left him to think that she merely wished to understand what was to her a new experience of intellectual powerlessness.

"Sometimes," said she, with a lack of conceit very pleasing to him, "I think I may have made a great blunder in thinking that I had the least talent for what I have undertaken; so that now I am waking up to a humiliating self-knowledge."

Her voice was low, as if she expected the confession would convince her hearer of its truth, and he would have to assure her that the scales were falling from her eyes. Still the minister was gentle, and she imagined she could endure the truth from him. He gave her confidence a genial laugh, by way of a first answer; then he said, "It is blue Monday with you, or it would be if you were a minister. I know what the trouble is: I think I do, at least. You have written for seven or eight years, have you not?"

"Yes, sir."

"Did you have literary friends to use their influence for you? or did you start unknown, and send your articles to strangers?"

"I had no such friends, knew no editors, never have had a patron, helper, or even a critical reader, to advise me what was good, bad, or indifferent, before I offered it for publication."

"You have always had your articles taken at good places, have you not? Critical editors have been willing to pay well for them, have they?"

"Oh, yes!"

"How could you victimize poor innocent men so, if you had no talent? What made them treat you as if you had? You must be a very artful blunderer in some way."

The quizzical words cheered Marion. It was rather inspiring to be so catechised by a minister; but she returned, "Well, perhaps I had some superficial talent. But, if I have worked myself out, what then?"

"Then you will have made a mistake that has been made before. But I do not think this is true. I will tell you how you can find out to the contrary perhaps. Lock up your writing-desk, — don't look at it for a long time; spend that time in finding out where there is a place as unlike any you have ever lived in as possible. Go off vagabondizing; delight yourself with out-of-the-way people and homes, and local living, thinking, and traditions. If you see something that interests you, pen-sketch it without a thought of what you will do with it. Find a new type of character, and study it psychologically. If you have never been in Europe, why not go? avoiding too persistently seeing the conventional sights, but finding the places you have never read about. Take time to get clear pictures in your mind; then come back and write stories, when it is a great deal easier for you to do so than it would be not to write them. You may go all around the world, and come home to find your very next-door neighbor a genuine inspiration, and the turnpike-road where you played as a child, a path into a rich region of fancy. Then you will probably wonder why you could not have saved your time and money, if you were not going to describe English lords and German peasants; but in time you will see that you needed tossing half across the earth to shake the dust out of your eyes, which prevents you from finding how clearly defined and interesting life is under your window. It is useless to try to see it so *now*. You are tired of it: you have nothing to put with it as a contrast. I think you are not written out: you need rest and change. I imagine, if you do not take my advice, you will"—

"What will I do?"

He looked at her with grave interest, then said, "I fear you will turn your eyes in, and study yourself, until you evolve morbid, intense novels. It is not well to consume one's self after that fashion. The end, too, is almost always failure."

"You are right, perhaps," answered Marion, "and what you say is encouraging and — discouraging."

She was silent a while, not explaining herself further, and then the conversation drifted toward other matters. She found Mr. Severn a restful companion. He was one of those people with whom, as Arthur Helps says, "you are supremely at ease, because the horrid idea will not cross your mind, 'What shall I say next?'" He was called away at last; and Marion, left alone, sank deeper into her easy-chair, reviewing the conversation in the twilight. "Vagabondizing a year in Europe! That is fine, indeed! I have heard one can get on nicely there only spending five dollars a day; for a year that is one thousand eight hundred and twenty-five dollars. I do not know how, in view of our circumstances, I could plan the tour, unless I mortgaged the house, sold the horse and cow, and put the family in the poor-house. It is a little too much to undertake: I had better wait until spring."

That evening Marion was agreeably surprised by the arrival of a copy of "The Phœnix" containing her last article, a check from the publishers, and a friendly letter from the editor. Granty ensconced herself by the drop-light with the fresh attractive journal, to see "what it was like;" while Dorothy, more interested in Mr. Craig's letter, asked, "Does he speak of seeing Hester?"

"Yes: he says she went to a fine private exhibition of pictures with him, and he thinks she must have enjoyed it very much."

"I should suppose she would have said she did."

"No," returned Marion. "If Hester imagines anybody expects her 'to extract ecstasy and paroxysm' out of any thing, as Sydney Smith says, that is the time she will be as unresponsive as a bell with the tongue taken out. Oh, those two must be very funny together! Mr. Craig never fails to have the right thought expressed in the choicest words, on the moment. Hester is as likely to make a prickly, ginger-snappy retort, as she also is to make no answer at all, when a response is breathlessly expected. How did she get along with Mr. Severn, Dorothy?"

"Just beautifully. I was astonished at her. They rode out together sometimes. He had calls to make on a sick old lady, his parishioner, six miles away. Hester took him; and I am not sure she did not prescribe for the woman every time she went. I know that once she put a bran-and-turpentine poultice, or plaster, or something of the sort, on her,—something I never heard of before, nor had Mr. Severn, either; for he amused her mightily by dropping his sermon the next day, and coming in to ask her if she was sure she knew what she was about when she advised it. Was it not explosive?"

Granty was a little shocked at the fun she poked

at him. She said it certainly would make trouble for the woman, if they set her on fire; but nevertheless she knew what she had done. Yes; she was never brusque with Mr. Severn, and he liked her."

"Dorothy," whispered Marion, with a glance toward Granty, who was not heeding them at all, — "Dorothy, I had an idea that Hester admired him very much. She wrote about him several times. It was strange for her to give half a page to any man."

Dorothy nodded emphatically, whispering, in return, "I know — I saw things myself. But it may be there was nothing in them; for you know Hester says we are none of us ever to marry."

"Indeed! Are we not free moral agents. I shall not ask permission of Hester, I assure you."

Dorothy was laughing when Granty put down the journal, saying, "That reads well, Marion. I would send them another, but have a better title."

"Why do you not like that title?" asked Marion, who had the greatest respect for Granty's literary taste. Her instincts were almost always unerring. The article she praised was sure to win approval when sent out; while her hints and criticisms had been of great value to the young writer.

The old lady answered her at length, then resumed her knitting.

"Dorothy, hear the wind blow!" she exclaimed.

"It is going to be a wild night. Did you tell Pete to give Old Mortality plenty of straw for his bed, and to see all the barn-doors were securely fastened?"

"Yes, Granty, I attended to it all before dark."

"I am seriously afraid that Buttercup is neglected, now Hester is away. I looked at her to-day; and it seemed to me she acted mournful, swung her tail as if she were uncomfortable: it had burs in it too; and that is a shame! Pete shall get them out, if he lives until to-morrow. Won't you charge your mind a little more with such things, girls? I am pretty old to have charge of an establishment like this: some old ladies, in my place, would do little more than read their Bibles, and take care of themselves."

"I know it, Granty; and we are very sorry to see you do so much," returned Dorothy. "You overtire yourself every day; but we cannot seem to prevent it."

"While I can, I prefer to attend to things myself, and then they are attended to. — Marion, you spoke of having my new black dress made this week. I don't know but I might as well have something more of a trail to it than the last one had. I noticed Mrs. Howells's, at our tea-party, was quite long. I don't wish to look bobbed off. There! I must go right out to the kitchen, and start Pete off with a basket of provisions for that poor, suffering Jones family. He is out of work, and is down with a fever."

"Let me do it for you," cried Dorothy; but she could only follow in the wake of the little lady, whose cap-strings were vanishing kitchenward. A few moments later, Marion overheard her charging Pete, with the half-motherly, half great-lady air so natural to her, "See if they have a fire, Pete; and tell them never to suffer for any thing, or to let the poor little children go without plenty of proper food, but to send one of them right up here with a basket. Don't you break that jelly-jar, or spill the milk."

"Dear little, old Lady Bountiful," thought Marion, "with generations of generous ancestors behind her, with the recollections of a long life clinging to her, may she never refrain from giving away the next to the last basketful she has! To the *very* last one she will never come: I am sure of that. God will not forget his own. Granty has been for seventy years a living gospel of love and good works, bound in a quaint cover perhaps, but a gospel just the same."

At this point Granty returned, and sent her peremptorily to bed, as if she were a giddy child of seven. She went to her room, but not at once to rest. She gazed again reproachfully at her writing-desk, as if it had served her some very shabby trick. She addressed it thus, "Why don't I write something that will be a great success, — a popular book?"

The question gave her a new impulse. She went

to a drawer, found, after a considerable search, a pile of old newspapers dated a few years back. They contained her one "sensation story." Slipped into the pages of the first chapter was a long envelope containing a paper stating that she obtained her copyright of the librarian of Congress at such a date. With newly awakened interest, Marion began to read the story itself slowly, critically, as if it had been written by another. It was an hour before she stopped, thinking, "If to-day I had given me those characters and those scenes, I could not write half so brilliant a story. The editor of 'The —— Gazette' offered to take as many in the same line as I should send him from time to time. I never had any desire to write another. I never have offered this, since then, to any publisher, although it attracted a good deal of attention in a paper very poorly adapted to bring it before the public. It is not weak at all: far poorer books have had a tremendous popularity for a season or so. I might get it republished as a summer novel. Why not?"

Why not? That was the question Marion argued and answered and re-argued, as if it were some sort of a temptation to be overcome rather than a simple business matter to settle, once for all, so far as she was concerned. If there was money in it, why not get money out of it? No: she could not put it that way simply. Judged by her sternest creed of literary faith, was it a poorly written book? No. She would have liked to stop there; but she was a child in regular generation of all those Puritans whose grave faces adorned the lower walls. Her eyes were as searching as theirs. Back of the writer, the white-souled woman was asking, "Will it be a good book for me to put my name to? Have I not gone beyond it now?"

"I wonder what Mr. Severn would say to it," she exclaimed at last. "It is not at all in Mr. Craig's line of work or thought. He would say, as some one else does, that, 'for those that like that sort of thing, it is the sort of thing they would like.' He might prune a little, and suggest a publisher. I wonder if Mr. Severn ever reads novels. That makes no difference: he can read this. He is candid and unprejudiced. I shall put it between him and his next sermon, and I believe I will accept his advice about republishing it. Meanwhile I will go to sleep."

CHAPTER XVII.

A Letter from Hester.

DEC. 20, 18—.

DEAR MARION, — I presume you think I write very few letters; but you, having been here so lately, know just how every thing goes; while I am so busy making the most of my time, that I forget to write. Each day, at night, I resolve to do so the next day, and neglect it. Aunt Pepperfield finds a great deal to do since she came back, and therefore leaves me to my own devices. Marion, — now I think to ask you, — won't you order me two stretchers covered with canvas? I want them when I get home. One I wish to be twelve by fifteen; the other, twenty by thirty-six. Then will you go over to the Eggerton farm, and get a quantity of pumpkins for Pete to feed to the cow, as I instructed him before I came away? The roads are so heavy now, that of course you do not use the phaeton: don't you think it a good time to send it to the carriage-maker's, and have it made thoroughly strong? The running-gear is out of order somewhere. There is one other thing: I waked up the other night, and grew very nervous thinking of our drainage. One pipe that runs out of the cellar is defective. I fear you will get the fever or diphtheria, unless it is all right. Have it looked to at once. I expect to be home in a week or ten days from now. I have seen all the picture-galleries and art-rooms, and have ransacked five or six old bookstores from top to bottom. I shall bring you some prizes. What do you say to a— Wait until you see it.

I find your friend Mr. Craig has been used to a paper-muslin kind of women, who are wilted by any exposure outside of a parlor. Undoubtedly I have shocked him terribly,—last week, for once, most effectually. One day when I was in the city, I saw a queer *white* wooden box on wheels, and was told that it was the "Black Maria," that took the sick to the free hospitals, the insane to the asylums, and the criminals to punishment. I asked Mr. Craig that same evening all about those places,—where they were, and so on. I received full and explicit information in regard to the "institutions of charity and correction," with many statistics, all in that gentleman's faultless style of conversation. Now, I had never been over a hospital in all my life; and it occurred to me instantly that I would like to see a monstrous institution of this sort, and I said so. He said no, I would not. I answered that I certainly *would*. I suppose it is the doctor in me, as you say; but it seems as if I do have the same kind of interest in sickness and suffering that uncle Jack had, and I am drawn to places where I know it is. Well, this autocrat of an editor said something about morbid curiosity that provoked me—as if I wanted just to look at suffering as a spectacle. I could not explain what I wished to go for; but it certainly was not that. I found out I must start from here quite early in the morning in order to get to the foot of —— Street, to take a boat for the islands. I must return, of course, in the afternoon. Now, a woman of my age and experience does not like to be told of trivial little unpleasantnesses, or to have people act as if any undertaking at all out of the usual line of sight-seeing was vaguely improper in mysterious ways. To be sure, I did not care to have aunt Pepperfield know where I was going; for she would make uncle Pepperfield go along with me, or else she would worry. Mr. Craig proposed that I should wait to have him for a companion. I did not need or want him: so I refused, and started off last Wednesday alone. When I arrived at the wharf, I asked if the boat which I saw there went to the particular hospital that I meant to visit; and I was told yes. So it did, but it stopped several times on the way. It stopped first at a great lunatic-asylum. I cheerily walked off a plank, and discovered my mistake when the steamer was puffing away far from shore, and a few lunatics besides myself were left behind. They all had attendants, however; and in this I was at a disadvantage. I asked one of these what was the sanest thing that I could do; and I was told to walk for a mile or more to the other end of this island, where I would find my hospital. If I did not wish to, there was an almshouse, a penitentiary, and, I believe, an idiot-asylum near, where I might find refuge. I walked; and I think it was the most exciting promenade I ever took. The path ran along by the water, in front of all these buildings; very conveniently situated, too, for me to jump in, if any one pursued me viciously. However, I enjoyed it; being only sorry that the clouds looked like rain. I met a group of women in Shaker-hats, sitting on the sunny side of a sort of summer-house, and one of them urged me to stay to tea. Poor creatures! I was hurrying along, when they shouted out to know if I could not sing. I suppose it was very absurd; but I sat down on an inverted wheelbarrow a little way off, and gave them "The Sweet By and By." They proposed to dance when I ended: so I went on, although I felt more at ease on the lunatics' ground than when I neared the penitentiary, where convicts in striped clothes were at work. I reasoned that there must be a guard around, and hurried along. After a long walk, I reached the great hospital,— a castle of misery, with great stone turrets against the sky. I shall tell you nothing of what I saw or heard until I get home. I did not think any thing about the time until three o'clock; then I heard that the boat would not be along again in an hour, having been already up and down once since I came. Now, I ought to have asked if it did not stop right there where I was; but, you see, I imagined that I must, of course, go back, and get on to it where I got off. I walked stupidly over the whole ground again, in a Scotch mist, which took all the curl out of my pretty brown hat-plume. I was no sooner at the landing than I discovered that my steamer had stopped away back at the hospital I had left, and now was puffing right away, down to the city, leaving me, Hester Prescott, high, but not dry, on the rocks in front of a mad-house, at five o'clock of a December afternoon. No one knew where I was. Aunt Pepperfield thought I had been sauntering through Schaus's or Goupil's. When the boat was out of sight, I thought it was all I could do decide whether I should ask shelter, for the time being, as idiotic, poverty-stricken, or insane. The latter concession to circumstances seemed the least humiliating: so I pattered up to a gloomy portal in a pair of very damp kid shoes, where I encountered a polite and quite rational doctor, to whom I told my tale, fearful that he would not believe it, but would pull a strait-jacket out of his pocket. No: he told me he could send me back to the hospital again, with an order which would enable me to cross the river in a tug-boat; then, landing up town, I could, by cross cars and stages, work my way to the ferry, and possibly get out to Ingleside by eight or nine o'clock in the evening. Perhaps you think I was sorry that I came. I was not at all. Well, this time I rode in my carriage,—a unique equipage with a lock and key. Its battered sides suggested that it had carried more uneasy passengers than I was. In a short time I took the tug-boat, which brought me safe across to an unfamiliar part of the city, where I was told to walk a few blocks, and find my car. It was getting almost dark, and I was very tired, when I discovered a man unmistakably following me, and that very fast. I dashed out into a crowd on the near avenue, and rushed into the car, which happily, as I thought, was on the spot. We started at once; but more trouble was to come. I was on the right car; but I did not get off at the right street. I went seventeen miles, more or less, out of my way, before I alighted, to discover the fact later. The first thing that I saw was an act of oppression which stirred my blood. You will laugh now: I did, after I was home. A street girl — a big, ungainly Arab, or Arabess — had pounced on a smaller one, laid her flat on the pavement, and was (as I thought) pulling out one of her teeth. I came to the rescue, and she bellowed that it was *her chewing-gum.* Well, the principle is the same. I seized the big girl by the arm, and exclaimed, "Give it back, right away! Aren't you ashamed?"

"*Sic semper tyrannis,*" said some one solemnly in my ear; and there, in his new ulster, with a big umbrella, and a roll of manuscript in each pocket, stood your Mr. Craig. He put the umbrella over me, offered his arm, and asked if it made any difference which way we went.

"Where did I seem to be going?" I asked.

"South by south-west, or directly toward the Tombs," he answered blandly.

I said it was too late for a visit there: I would go home, instead. I wonder, if you had been as tired, as hungry, had felt so like a fool, as I did then, you would have liked to consider how proper, aristocratic, and almost like a stranger, this man was of whom you must ask the way home. He is a gentleman. He only said, "You are in a puzzling part of the city:

I am very glad I found you." Then, as bluntly as uncle Pepperfield would have taken care of me, he asked, "Have you had any thing to eat since morning? I know you have not. I am very hungry myself. We shall not get into Ingleside before nine o'clock: so let us get some coffee and oysters. There is a quiet, neat little restaurant near here: let us find it."

On the way to the ferry, I asked him how he came to be on the spot where I alighted from the cars. He said he went early in the afternoon to the foot of —— Street, to meet me on my return to the city. When he found I had missed the last boat, he asked what I would probably do, and was told of the tugboat, in which he could go across and find me, if he first rode up town. He did so, and did not have to go across; for at the boat he learned a lady had just been brought over, and was walking up the block. He turned, followed quickly, and saw me enter a car. He caught the next one, and, standing in front, could watch me, and tell when I got out. It was he from whom I ran away; but I did not tell him that. I was grateful to him for taking so much trouble, although he made nothing of it; and, whatever he thought, he did not imply in words that I had done any thing singular. He only asked if I was glad I had gone, and I said yes; for now I know exactly how poor little Jim Welles ought to be treated for his deformity. He need not suffer one-half the pain he has. One of the doctors had a similar case in the hospital; and, after I asked a few questions, he described his treatment to me in detail. Tell Jim's mother to stop what she was doing when I came away, and wait until I get home. I have learned a great deal from that one visit. The coffee must have excited me; for I told Mr. Craig all my experiences, and talked until he must have been amazed. However, I do not think I have said ten words to him since then: so that is atoned for. We were home before nine, and Mr.

Craig passed it off as nothing strange. He said he met me in town, and we were belated. Of course, I told aunt Pepperfield all about it the next day. She turned pale, and went away and fumigated all my clothes. Yesterday she said she had read they "had the leprosy over there." She was relieved to learn that it was not on exhibition, if "there" at all. . . .

CHAPTER XVIII.

Whose Rose Was It?

MR. SEVERN was glad that he had been in the habit of writing his sermons in the early part of the day, and taking his evenings for any occupation that suited him best. Now, it was very natural that he should join the social family circle that usually formed itself about the centre-table in the library, these long evenings of the early winter. Sometimes he read to the rest, a few pages at a time, with long digressions, often started by Granty, whose keen eyes twinkled over her glittering knitting-needles. She could be busy with them, yet alert enough to follow every page read. Jack and the old cat, in a tender embrace, would sit at his feet; but even these listeners might not have been satisfying, had the young ladies been absent. It was inspiring to Mr. Severn to have Dorothy make her good-natured comments, or to look up and see Marion's eyes fixed on the glowing coals, her own thoughts sent all abroad by some suggestive sentence. He always knew, too, if Hester was there, if she did not once speak. He had found out what books she liked, and divined her opinions on many things of which she never talked. People who knew Hester for any length of time always did understand her aright, if they were the kind of people whose appreciation signified at all. The tone in which she said, "Humph," after some exquisite poem, for instance, was as expressive as an effusion of sentiment from somebody else; while her longer utterances were remembered when blander ones might be forgotten.

Since his theological-seminary days, Mr. Severn had not given himself in any marked degree to ladies' society. At that period of his life he had been shy, but not unsusceptible: later, work, travel, and books had kept him from matrimony. A few weeks of life in the Howells family had made him think his tastes must be those of a recluse, and that old Thomas à Kempis was shrewd, as well as pious, in dismissing the subject with "commend all good women in general to the Lord."

A few months here had wrought a change. He was like a boat long snugly moored, but by secret agencies gradually made free, and sent adrift, fanned by quite new breezes, shaken by currents unfelt before. What would Dorothy have thought, or Hester, or Marion, had they known that he returned from a call one evening, and found in the hall a tiny white Christmas rose dropped by one of them? The rose went up to the minister's room: the thoughts it stirred into a poem that nobody ever saw, nor was it meant for sight. Dorothy did take note of his increasing interest in them all as a family. By common consent, uncle Jack's office had been given up to a worker, the minister, and the skeleton. The singular trio spent much time there in perfect harmony. One half the room, quite shut in by a folding-screen, contained pills and powders, medical briefs, surgical instruments, phials, bottles, ledgers, and, in turn, Dorothy's account-books, Marion's manuscripts, and Hester's easel. The minister's half, quite secluded also, was his study; and beyond, in its silken drapery, was the third, the silent partner, who disturbed none of the others.

One afternoon Marion was quietly sitting by uncle Jack's writing-desk, when Mr. Severn, from behind the partition, said, "May I come in there for a while?"

"Certainly," she responded, arising to turn around an enormous wooden chair that filled one corner of the room, its arms hospitably extended to welcome a giant.

"I can never, with propriety, say I will take that chair," he said, entering through the hall; "but, so far as I go, I will let it take me."

He seated himself; and Marion saw in his hand the roll of papers whose return she had expected with some anxiety. He talked of indifferent matters, until she asked directly, "If you were me, would you republish that story in book-form?"

"Do not put a question to me in that way; for I cannot answer it. I do not know you as I ought. I should have to know your motive in publishing any book."

"My chief motive in publishing this would be to make money."

He had not expected such an answer, and he looked disappointed. But he answered, "Then, if I know any thing about one kind of success, I think you would succeed, — would make money, as you say."

Marion looked past him out of the window, with the earnest, unworldly look in her refined face, — the look well known to him, — that had made her mercenary words have almost the shock of vulgarity.

"I do not want money because I love it, or because I ever wrote for the sake of it before. I never did. Only I wish it now," she said, looking in his face. And he gladly believed her when she added, "But, all that aside, I shall not republish this if it is not a good book. What do you think of it?"

"From a dramatic point of view, it is excellent. It

has unity; is very spirited. Its delineations of passion are intense, but not overdrawn. It is exceedingly witty. You have shown power in casting scenes that are natural, and in portraying characters which are lifelike, especially when one reflects that you can *never have been in such society, or known intimately such persons.* You read a few French novels before you wrote this story; not many (for it is not an imitation), but enough to know by artistic intuition what lives wholly apart from your own were like. I find it different in every respect from your other writings, and as unlike *you.* It has certainly some remarkable merits."

Mr. Severn stopped, as if he had said all he wished to say, and yet not all he would say. The color in Marion's cheek had not deepened by a tint at his words. She was no tremulous young girl with her first book. She knew how her story had impressed others, as good judges of literary work as Mr. Severn. She was not surprised at what she had heard before, and it did not occur to her to feign surprise. She went deeper than before, saying, "Tell me, Mr. Severn, if you think this is a good book, judged by your ideas of a good one."

"I shall not answer you in character as a minister, remember, but simply as a man. Some of the truest, noblest books I have ever read have not any 'religion,' as the word goes, from title-page to end. I do not demand that a book of fiction be pious: I only think it should stand a few tests to be called 'good.'"

"What tests?" asked Marion promptly. His eyes had a sorry expression, as if he wished he were back the other side of the screen, instead of sitting here, making this gentle young woman look at her papers as severely as if saying, "Come up to the judgment-seat, and stand or fall!" She wanted money for good reasons probably; and if he went on he might be, figuratively, picking her pockets. He smiled, with a futile attempt to evade her by saying, "My tests would not be your tests if I were in your place; but I should have yours: so the question now really is, what yours are."

"Not so," she answered. "My question is of yours, and you have not yet answered it."

He waited a moment, then asked, "If all your stories but one must be unwritten, would you choose this for the fittest?"

"No."

"Why not? Or may I ask if it is not for one reason,—that it is not a real expression of yourself? A writer's best book ought to be that. I do not think you could have told this story better; but it is not a good story for you to tell. You have been delicate, artistic, vaguely suggestive, when you could not have been definite without being coarse. Another telling this same story would have left out half-tints, put in details, and the book would have been morally bad. It only failed to be, because, there being too little evil in you for the purpose, you innocently made it brilliant instead of wicked. The first page will hold the reader; the whole story will fascinate him or her: but nobody will be stronger, more hopeful in self, more helpful to others, for such fiction. You may here detect the preacher in me, and for your part believe that stories are best when morally purposeless, if only well written. If you do, I can only repeat that this story *is* effective and original: it may be a popular success. I sat up half a night to read it, and had a headache all the next day. Can I give you a stronger proof that it is interesting?"

"I think myself that it is not stupid," said Marion, laughing, and rolling the papers into a tighter bundle.

He was glad to detect no resentment in her tone, or any look of wounded vanity in her face. She arose, and drew back the curtain to let in the glow of a brief winter sunset; then she turned, and without any ceremony dropped the roll of papers back in the hottest coals of the grate, saying, with a laugh, " Have you ever heard of the little boy who declared that 'pins had saved thousands of lives by *not* being swallowed'? On the same principle, perhaps, you have saved scores of people from vexation of spirit, Mr. Severn. This great success of a book (we will believe it would have been) might have been the one to be peddled on the cars all summer, to be thrust into tired travellers' faces by troublesome agents. Now we prevent all that by its not being published."

"I am not at all sure they would thank me if they knew what I had done," said he half ruefully. "You did not tell me I was to be the ultimate authority. You only asked my opinion."

"And I should not have accepted it, if it had not seemed right in my own eyes. I thank you very much for reading the story, and am sorry it gave you a headache. You should not have sat up so late: a minister who preaches moderation should practise it in novel-reading."

"A minister is just like any other man," returned Mr. Severn, leaning back in the great chair, and thinking a layman or priest watching Marion, with the yellow light on her brown hair, her graceful figure, and dainty dress, — any man would wander in thought from the woman's work to the lovable woman herself. Mr. Severn's fancies did, and not for the first time. It was also perhaps reprehensible in him, after spoiling her pecuniary prospects as he had, that he heard her with positive pleasure, when later she said, "I have concluded, Mr. Severn, that I cannot go 'vagabondizing' about Europe for a long time to come. I must stay at home for several reasons."

"I am glad," he answered.

She looked up surprised, and met a gleam from his eyes, which caused her afterwards to reflect that kindly people, when they happen to have fine eyes, may seem to express therewith much more warmth of sympathy than there is any reason to suppose they feel. At the time she was embarrassed. There seemed a new subtile something in her companion's tone and manner; or was she fanciful in that half mystical light of the gloamin' that lingered after the day? Their conversation had been practical; but, when the subject-matter of it was reduced to ashes, Mr. Severn did not return to his sermon. Marion wondered; but she rather enjoyed having him neglect the spiritual interests of his parishioners, in a mild fashion of course.

Presently, down the hall came an approaching whistle, so loud, so shrill, so windy, the mystery was that Jack ever got it well under way without exploding in the process. He blew it off, however, before he banged the office-door with a crash that set the silent partner into a dismal agitation, and made the minister cry, "Alas, poor Yorick! Have mercy on him, Jack!" Then he arose, and, reaching out his hand, said, "I hope you will not be sorry you asked me to read the story."

Marion gave him her hand a second, saying, "You were sincere enough to tell me the truth, and I had sense enough to receive it. There can be nothing to regret."

"Supper is ready," said Jack. "Didn't you hear the bell?"

They heard, and obeyed it a moment after.

"Is Mr. Severn going back to board at the Howells'?" asked Jack very abruptly that night of Marion, as she was bidding him good-night in his room.

"Why, no. Why do you ask?"

"Oh, nothing! Only, when he was shaking hands in the office, he looked — looked like folks do when they aren't going to see their friends very often."

"'Like folks do' is an incorrect expression," said Marion, smiling in the dark. "As folks do, you should say."

Then the light was turned up that Jack might see if any ghosts or stray wild animals from African jungles were lurking behind washstand or bureau. There were none; and he slept in peace.

CHAPTER XIX.

A Watch in the Night.

"ANOTHER 'Phœnix' office letter!" cried Jack, prancing into the library, and dropping it into Hester's lap, as she sat reading by the table.

"The second one this week. What does he write about?" asked Dorothy.

"I could tell better, if he wrote to me," answered Hester, studying the bold chirography. "I think he has accepted another article, and writes to Marion about a change in it."

"Well," said Granty, who was very shrewd in times when one least expected her to be, "I think he writes longer letters to her, and oftener, than editors with whom she has had far more business. She has had but two articles before this in 'The Phœnix.'"

"His being an intimate friend of the Pepperfields' makes a difference; and he knows Marion well," said Dorothy.

"And you too, Hester. Did you like him?"

"Yes."

"As well as you like — as we all like Mr. Severn?"

"Yes. They are men not at all alike."

"How do they differ?" asked Dorothy.

Hester answered, "Marion says, if a man insulted Mr. Severn in his study, he would say, 'Go!' The look in his eyes would send him over the threshold. Mr. Craig would make a remark he would remember, but make it with a grip on his collar. There is fight in both of them; but one would go into a contest with fate hot and heavy, and compel the issue: the other would endure much. Either might be a general, but only Mr. Severn could be a martyr."

"Well," continued Granty, "from some things Jack has told me from time to time, I judge the interest Mr. Craig took in Marion last summer was rather marked. Do editors usually go beech-nutting with their lady-contributors, and lend them the newest books? To be sure, it was natural enough. Marion is young yet, and very good-looking. I am not sure *Mr. Severn* does not enjoy our society better than he did before she returned."

"It will do him no good," returned Hester. "Marion will never marry a minister."

"No, not if he were made of gold, and studded all over with diamonds — or so she told me once," remarked Granty, making Jack hunt for one of her knitting-needles. When it was found, she took him to bed, leaving Hester and Dorothy together.

"Do you think there is any thing in this notion of Granty's about Mr. Craig?" asked Dorothy.

"I cannot tell," answered Hester sharply. "Perhaps there is. If he is not one to be pleased with every woman he meets in that way, and to show the admiration a man had better keep to himself, unless he means it to be seen for a purpose, I do not understand him."

Dorothy secretly wondered if what Granty had said of Mr. Severn had in any way jarred on Hester. Then she fell to musing on changes in the domestic atmosphere of late. It seemed to her new elements had been introduced; and she was not mistaken. For several years previous to this, these young women had painted and written, and kept house, had petted little Jack, and cared for uncle Jack, had not in all that time talked much or thought more of men or marriage. Now, not one of them was engaged, not one of them in love (unless the malady was deep-seated and occult); yet the proposal of Mr. Scudder, or the introduction of Mr. Severn, or the acquaintance of the editor of "The Phœnix," or all of these together, had worked a change.

As Hester painted, she asked herself, "What if things are thus or so?" When Marion tried to write stories with "warmth enough of sentiment to suit a love-liking public," she found herself shading them off into vagueness which was sure to be displeasing to people who wanted every detail clear. As for Dorothy, she had actual and romantic work on hand. Mr. Scudder held such amicable interviews with her, that Granty was puzzled, especially as " he had begun going to the Howells' two or three times a week;" or so she affirmed. The truth was, that, since the day that Dorothy took Molly to look at his farm, Mr. Scudder's mind had been settled as to the person whom he desired for the future Mrs. Scudder. His way was hedged in at first : a less determined suitor would have lost the day. He wore such gay ties and fine vests, so many charms on his watch-chain, that Miss Maude made endless fun of him. Molly was kind-hearted, and, feeling guilty because she laughed also, she endeavored to treat him with more cordiality. To this end, she drew him on to talk of what he best understood, and after a while was herself interested in his farm and in his plans. She unwittingly improved him; and his attire grew simpler, his manner quieter. The result was not surprising to Dorothy. Molly was tired of her life of inaction: she saw another, in which was abundant promise of activity and independence. There was no sentimentality in Molly: she had no *beau idéal* of a husband to banish before she could begin to like Mr. Scudder when once she saw his genuine good qualities. For a while Mrs. Howells was at her wits' ends to know where among her bric-a-brac, her old china and Japanese fans, her screens and antique jugs, to find a place for this big provincial curiosity.

We greatly fear he never would have been allowed to rest his elbows in her embroidered sofa-cushions, or put his head against her Turkish chairs, had it not been for his wide-stretching acres. As it was, he came until he conquered; and Molly confessed to Dorothy she preferred hearing about his farm, his children, and his neighbors, to opera music or talk about art. She avowed that she hated "aht."

So, also, Mr. Scudder one day appeared in a new and faultless suit of clothes, and to Dorothy told the fact of his engagement to Miss Mary Howells. He asked for Hester, and bashfully informed her that he would be delighted if she would now paint Molly, "thrown up as big as ever was done or heard of, no matter what it cost."

Hester labored to convince him that a picture less than life-size would be better than one larger, and he departed radiant. The crowning blessing was to be added to his life, with another gem to his collection of family portraits.

But to return to Dorothy. This evening, as she sat alone with Hester, she asked, "How are you getting on with Molly's picture? Better, I hope, than Marion does with her writing."

"It will be a very handsome picture when done," said Hester. "In a free, large way, Molly is a beauty. I think she will be in her element when she is living in the country. She always looks too big and too natural for her home. No: I shall not fail while I have pictures like this to paint; for the work is largely mechanical. But I am getting tired: I would like to stop, and" —

"Go to Europe!" put in Dorothy in desperation, — "go vagabondizing and zig-zagging?"

"Yes. Or to begin studying art, really studying it in the way I have come to see I ought. What I am doing now, merely to earn money, is unworthy" —

"Oh, dear me! Unworthy of what?"

"Well, not of myself; for I am doing it from the best motives. But after studying really fine pictures, learning what conscientious workers are doing, I feel like a dauber, — a well-meaning one, but a dauber, nevertheless."

"Well, well," said Dorothy bluntly, "I wish both of you had staid at home! Marion questions her talent for writing: you are only painting mechanically. As for me, I am also losing enthusiasm in my occupation, which is mainly to make five dollars do the same that ten dollars did in palmier days. Hester, tell me what the end is going to be! I don't enjoy economy: it seriously interferes with all my plans."

Hester looked grimly at the portrait of a great-uncle who had squandered a fortune, and said nothing, only scowled, as if asking him why he did it; then she arose abruptly, and went about her task of locking the house for the night. This was a task not lightly accomplished; for, no matter how long before Granty may have retired, she issued forth, aroused by some instinct that told her what Hester was about. She must be assured that no sparks could fly from the fireplaces, that no cat was in the house, and that the dog was; that Bridget had mixed the buckwheat-cakes, and the milk was where it would not sour. Last of all, Hester must warn Mr. Severn not to leave matches in his papers, lest the house be set on fire. She always attended herself to these same things; but this was a test applied later for greater security. To-night Hester knew that Mr. Severn was not in the office: so she went to cover the fire in the grate, and to put out the gas. She went for that purpose, but she lingered. Finding the quiet room attractive, she sat down to think in uncle Jack's great chair. It was not mere discontent, or the fear of poverty, that made Hester, as she sat there, turn over in her mind Dorothy's words, "Tell me what the end s going to be." Of late many thoughts had come to her: she was not satisfied with the measure of her progress, if, indeed, she made any progress, in her favorite art. The necessity of earning money crippled her at the outset. She must paint what she could sell, not what she was coming surely to realize were the subjects she ought to attempt for her own best culture. Back still of this was the knowledge, that, *even if she could* cultivate her tastes to the utmost, the result here would be, Hester Prescott, a good copyist. She had not the genius which is a law unto itself, which makes a man or a woman say, in the face of all difficulties, " Woe be unto me, if I use not the gift that is in me!" She wished that she could draw and paint in the future as once in the past, — taking brush or pencil as she liked, putting them down when the mood changed. Not that Hester had not an earnest nature. She had just that; and now, in the full prime of young womanhood, she felt that whatever became an end in her life must absorb her whole enthusiasm and energy; that, it being her work, she must do it in her very best way. She was not so painting: she could not so paint, and she knew it. Therefore to-night, as she sat putting questions to herself, what wonder she was cast down? that, in looking out on the future, she feared a poverty which had something worse in it than any that concerned her outer circumstances, — the poverty of an inner life that misses the mark, — its mark? Her sister Marion's doubts of herself were clouds over a sky where the sun did surely shine; but Hester felt that she herself was going on in a way that grew gloomier, — not a wrong way, because it seemed to her the only way, but one at the end of which she saw failure. Yet what could be done? The lines were cast for her. She had no time to speculate, to build castles like a young girl, even to be blue. The shadows danced up and down among the medical books; the lights played over Hester while she sat long by the big desk, her head bent, her hands on the old chair-arms, just where the doctor's toil-worn ones had rubbed them bare of paint. At last she arose, and, crossing the room, opened the glass doors of a case as the clock struck midnight. Often before, when Hester felt as to-night, she had gone and looked at what she called "our inheritance." On a shelf in one corner were a pile of dusty, leather-covered books, each lettered, "Physician's Day-Book." One looked much like another; for all were full of uncle Jack's close writing in pencil, — names and names and names of people! A strange, softened awe crept over Hester when she thought what those names stood for, — pains and groans and agony; stood for patients of uncle Jack, who, scattered far and wide, remembered him as a Great Heart, who fought battles for them with death itself, and conquered; stood for others, who, like him, had gone quite beyond, and left only names behind. She wondered if, in that to her dim land, he had yet met them, and talked of this now behind them forever. One thing she always saw with shining eyes, — a tiny cross over scores of these old names. That stood for the time, care, skill, and knowledge, for which he expected no return in earthly coin. Each word meant to Hester, as she stood slowly picking them out, that on the year and day when the old man's feet crossed such and such a threshold was a time that the voice no more heard cheered some sufferer who also had since ceased suffering. Yes, this was Hester's inheritance, — the record of fifty years of work for and loving-kindness to men, women, and little children. When she pushed the day-books back, and locked the desk, she had lost the thought of poverty. She looked as if she might have been reading a psalm.

Surprised to find the hour so late, Hester was going immediately to her own room, when there came a hurried rap on the office-door, and a voice she knew to be Molly Howells's said, "Open the door, please, Hester. We saw a light here, and your shadow on the curtain. Mother sent me to see if you could come over and help us."

"What is the matter?" asked Hester, opening it quickly to find Molly alone.

"Oh! grandmother has been sick for a good while, you know,— feverish, out of her mind a little, and sleepless. The doctor came about dark, said she did not need any change of medicine, and asked us not to send for him before to-morrow, unless it was very necessary. We do not think she is worse; but we cannot quiet her, and mother is all worn out. To-night she declares that the Devil, a dog, and an Episcopal minister, are in the room, and we are cruel that we will not put them out. The doctor left something to soothe her; but mother is not sure about his directions, and dare not give her much of it. You are as good as a doctor, Hester, and mother would be so glad to have you come in a little while!"

Hester caught up an "afghan" from the sofa, gave a low whistle that brought the great dog Lion, and followed Molly out into the clear starlight. Very little has been said of the domestic life of these neighbors, for the reason that they have little to do with the story. Here let it be mentioned that Mrs. Howells's mother had long been a member of the family. Of late she had been constantly ill, as Hester knew before Molly told her: she was therefore not surprised to be called in at this time. She followed Molly into the house to a pleasant room furnished with the old lady's possessions, dearer to her than the modern elegancies of the rest of the house. In one corner was a big bed, and, propped up in it, a little white grandmother, with restless black eyes, and withered little hands that fluttered frantically as she chattered, reproaching poor Mrs. Howells, who was at her wits' ends. With the best intentions, she had followed the worst course possible, and argued half the night to prove to the old lady that there was no dog, no Devil, no minister of any church whatever, there. She assured Hester that she felt half crazy herself.

"Well, now let me try my hand. Where is the medicine you dare not give?"

"Here it is. He said it was a powerful opiate, or anodyne, or something of that sort," answered Mrs. Howells nervously. "I meant to remember, but I can't for the life of me."

Hester calmly smelt and tasted it, regarding Mrs. Howells over the teaspoon. She was so grotesque, in a toilet for once nondescript,— her front hair in crimping-pins, her back hair missing.

"Chloral," said Hester. "I can give it to her."

"Well, do. She won't take a thing from me now; for I have tried her with every thing else I could think of that could not hurt her, or that might help her. She threw the last on the floor. — Peppermint, wasn't it, Molly?—Poor mother! she is not like herself nowadays."

"Of course not," said Hester. "Leave her to me now a while."

She lowered a window to cool the overheated room, then went to the bed with a hearty, "Nothing is going right, is it, grandmother?"

"No, it is not. Tell me I don't know a dog when I can see it!" whimpered the poor old lady; "and a minister, and the Devil in pink breeches, with a cardinal frock-coat and two rows of horn buttons. I do, now!"

"Certainly you do. If you *have* seen them, you know it, and they shall go out. Sit up a little straighter, and tell me where they are. Let us take the dog first."

At Hester's inspiring sympathy the old lady raised herself on her elbow, like a child who triumphs at last. Hester, standing before the door, softly turned the knob, and forthwith, as she had provided for, there was a dog in the room of the biggest, blackest sort. She let him approach the bed, let grandma cry, "See him now! see him!" then, with apparent ado, he was ejected, and the old lady clung to Hester in a rapture of gratitude. In a minute, however, she remembered the other intruders.

"If the Devil is here," said Hester, like one who

submits her judgment to another's, yet suggests a plan that may be feasible, "don't you think we had better confine him? If we turn him loose in the neighborhood, what work he may make before morning! Shut into the coal-scuttle now, with the shovel on top of him, he might stop his capers; or, so far as I am concerned, I would put him in the coal-stove itself. He is used to the temperature, and might stay there contentedly."

"If the ising-glass windows are tight, pop him right in," cried the invalid, with a little giggle of pleasure delightful to hear after her fretting. With due alacrity, Hester skirmished about the place, and returned to declare positively there was no stranger in the room unless it was the minister.

"Yes, yes! He is over there, with his surplice on hindside before, and a prayer-book in each hand."

"Indeed!" murmured Hester. "Well, it is a cold night to turn him out of doors. Are you a Christian, grandmother?"

"Of course!" answered the old lady with comical dignity; "a member of the Dutch Reformed Church for forty years."

"Then I would just let him read prayers down in the parlor, — prayers for the sick, you know. You don't feel well yet. Let me straighten you out on the pillows. There, how cool and sweet the air is here now!"

The old lady fell back in the pillows, pleased at the masterful, cheery tones. Hester brought the medicine, and in a moment of soothing talk, without a question or request, put it to her lips, and had it down as a thing of no account.

Mrs. Howells hovered about, out of sight, and in less than a half-hour the poor grandmother was quietly sleeping. Then Mrs. Howells, at Hester's orders, went to get a little rest herself. Molly insisted on staying with Hester. One took possession of the sofa, the other dozed in a great easy-chair.

"Who taught you so much about nursing and medicine?" asked Molly. "Or, rather, how came you to learn so much? Of course, your uncle taught you."

"Yes. He did not undertake to do it systematically; but when he found I listened to all he said about his patients, and asked questions, he gave me books to read, — the first, a little work on physiology, when I was only eight years old. There was never a day in which I did not learn something almost without design."

"Do you always know what to do?"

"I always know if I understand a simple ailment, and can tell what will help a person; or I know that I do *not* understand the disease, or complication of diseases, and must do nothing in ignorance. I have the greatest desire to know when I do *not* know, — to have the study and experience that would give me insight. I could get it much easier than it comes to some persons. Uncle Jack used to say I could enter a medical college in advance of any beginner."

"Why don't you? Why not study medicine, and take your uncle's practice?"

Getting no answer, Molly thought her companion sleepy, and fell asleep herself. The old lady in the bed slumbered peacefully as a baby. The wind arose, and blew about the house, and up and down the chimney, the fire burning as fiercely as if the demon were really stirring it up within; but Hester Prescott, wide awake, sat and seemed to watch the shadow of grandmother's night-cap on the wall.

"Why do you not study medicine, and take your uncle's practice?"

It was strange that nobody before had ever put the question. Over and over again she had been told that she should have been a man, then she would have made just as good a doctor as her uncle.

To-night, as she sat there in the sick-room, all the thoughts of the evening thronged back upon her; then she saw her future, by imagination, in a quite new light for the moment; saw herself as she "might be," — a power in the world, not spending her days trying to make the pretty, incomplete efforts of one mere accomplishment stand her in stead of a simple, grand work that would bring into action all the forces of her nature. The question was not for her vaguely put, "Will you try and become what perhaps a woman may be?" it was just this, "Wil' you become what you *know* that you can be?"

Indeed, it was not so much a question as a call coming to her in the fulness of time.

CHAPTER XX.

"What is decreed must be, and be this so."
SHAKSPEARE.

A FEW days after the night which Hester spent at the Howells's, she called Marion into her painting-room, and the two were a long time in conversation. At last Marion came out, and went in search of Dorothy, whom she found sewing alone in the warm and sunny dining-room. She was singing to herself in a hilarious way that she had when it was likely that her spirits were not at all in accordance with her high notes. But it was as easy to sing glees as dirges; and the effect was happier upon other people.

"What do you think now?" asked Marion, dislodging the sleek old cat from a chair, and taking it herself. "Hester is going to take up the kaleidoscope of our family affairs, and give it a great shake. She has amazed me with a new set of ideas. What do you think she is going to do?"

"Paint a panorama, perhaps, and wants you to write a lecture to go with it," suggested Dorothy.

"She says that she thinks it is very likely she will never paint any more after this year."

Dorothy dropped her work, a thought flashing across her mind. "She is not — Mr. — Well, what is it?"

"She says she is going to study medicine."

"She always has done it. She knows now more than she has any occasion to use."

"But she is going to practise — going to be a doctor — going to take uncle Jack's practice."

"Nonsense!" cried Dorothy, rapidly changing base in view of this information. "She going to start off on the *little* she knows! Why, a doctor must have attended college, lectures, studied anatomy, dissected, had hospital clinics, graduated, before having a diploma even. She will make a fool of herself. The regular profession would laugh her to scorn; and I should think uncle Jack's opinion of quacks would hinder her from making us all ridiculous."

"Don't you suppose she knows all that, Dorothy? She would never begin practising until she was thoroughly prepared. She says, however, she believes that she could enter on the second year" —

"Enter?" echoed Dorothy. "Where, and how? There are no colleges near here."

"But there are in the city. I thought, as you do, that Hester was wild, when she began to tell me. But let me show you what she means. You know, without any telling, what a passion she has for such things, and that, if she were a man, everybody would say she was made for a doctor. Now, here is a medical library, office, instruments, the good-will of all uncle Jack's old patients, who know and believe in her. It would be quite different if she were a visionary girl, starting up to enter on a career of which she knew nothing, and where she must struggle for any vantage-ground."

"But the time for preparation, and the expense, Marion," said Dorothy impatiently. "She cannot fit herself here."

"She knows that."

"Then, what is she thinking of?"

"I will tell you, if you will give me a chance. She says she will first write to uncle Jack's old friend, Dr. Willard, state her case in detail, and ask his advice. He can tell her of the best colleges to which women are admitted, and also, if one should apply for admission who was well advanced in preliminary studies, if she could get on and out sooner. All about fees and expenses, too, she must know, of course."

"And when she finds out," put in the irrepressible Dorothy, "how is she better off? She has not money enough for them. If she had, meanwhile what will she eat and drink, and wherewithal be clothed, in a strange city?"

"Well," returned Marion, a little chilled by these matter-of-fact questions which Hester had touched, it is true, but merely as subordinate issues (with her the one question had been, Shall I do it? not How can I?) "she says she should enter a medical college next fall. She could then have this year previous to that time for earning the money; and she could do it, she thinks. She would study evenings, but paint in the daytime more constantly than ever; perhaps take a few pupils in drawing. When the time comes, she would make an arrangement with aunt Pepperfield to remain with her during the time necessary for her college course. You know how she is always begging her to come there, and study art, because they are so near the city. She could go in and out every day. As for us, we must be more economical than we have been."

"Try it," said Dorothy dryly.

"I know. But the thing that ought to be done is always the thing that can be done. We might take a few summer-boarders when summer comes, — the house is large enough, — nice, quiet people. I would make any sacrifice; for I believe, if Hester had a medical education, she would be very successful. You know that, Dorothy, as well as I do, don't you?"

"Yes. If ever anybody was born to be a nurse and a doctor, Hester was; but I cannot endure women-doctors! Can you, Marion? I never had a bit of faith in them, had you?"

"No," answered Marion scornfully. Then in a moment each laughed at her own inconsistency.

"However," added Marion, "we know that Hester has now more knowledge and more skill, and quicker intuitions, than many newly-fledged doctors ready to kill or cure. She has a lifetime of study with a practising physician to match against their new experience of half-hours in hospitals. If we know that now, we will surely have faith in her when she has the fullest study required of them. Again: she is a true lady, if an odd one. I would like to see the person who would doubt that, even if she were a doctor."

"What will Granty say? There never was one among those Boston persons related to her who adorned her name with M.D. Granty may not think it proper."

"We must convert her, or else approach her with tact," returned Marion. "If some one like Mr. Severn should advocate the plan of having women study medicine, some women, at least, do it in a general way, let her think of it as something laudable, often desirable, and "—

"But gentlemen seldom like the idea. Mr. Severn may be greatly opposed to it."

Marion had not thought of this. A shadow fell on her face, and she murmured, —

"Yes. It might be eminently genteel for us to live along, Hester dabbling in colors, never able even to do the art work she might at her best, and at the most earning not much. But it seems to me that for her to enter a profession where she can be a helper in the world and at the same time can earn an ample support, — that seems far better than semi-helpless gentility. You know that a woman as a physician gets the same fees a man does. With a proper collection of bills, Hester can be what uncle Jack might have been, but never was, rich."

"She will be just what he was, — just precisely as easy-going," said Dorothy. "But even so there would always be enough, and plenty to spare. Yes. I wonder what Mr. Severn will say. I have fancied he liked her particularly well. If she studies medicine, I suppose she will never marry. She could not. Her time would be no longer her own; and no man would want a woman of whom that was true. But then Hester would not have made a good wife for a minister anyway."

"Yes," said Marion, "she said so; or she said, rather, it was as unnecessary to say it as for the man to say he would not live always when nobody had asked him to. Mr. Severn has not talked much with her lately."

"Suppose you sound him yourself, and see if he would be a good one to deal with Granty. When a thing has two handles, much depends upon the one she takes hold of first."

"Very well, I will."

The conversation was interrupted by Granty, who entered, panting from some unusual exertion, and sat down to recover breath."

"Oh, dear!" she exclaimed speedily. "I do wish you would write a book, Marion, all about boys, — trying little hired boys like Pete. There he drove that poor horse to Barnegat, last week, without any shoe on one foot: now he has a big corn, or something like it, in consequence, and Hester is in the barn soaking it in a pail of hot water."

"Which one has the corn and the hot water? — Pete, or the horse?" asked Dorothy.

"Why, Old Mortality; and his hair is all rubbed the wrong way, and looks rough as an old buffalo-skin. It makes me feel sorry to see him so neglected — and he is very unreliable. If I send him to Wilkins's for oysters, where they keep the best, he goes to Jones's, because it is nearer, and gets those that smell fishy. He is saucy to Bridget, and then gets ugly because she loses patience, and calls him 'A dirty black African race,' as if there were ever so many of him. I'm sure one is enough. There! I forgot to tell Hester his last dreadful caper, — his and Jack's together. I should admire to know what she will think of it."

"What was it, Granty?" asked Marion, helping the old lady extricate herself from a voluminous white cloud wrapped over her head and shoulders.

"Well, they wanted to make a fountain, and have the spray look like that at Niagara. So what did they do but go into the office, and search until they found a stomach-pump, and cut it up, and got ever so many rubber tubes they found there, to tie together some way? Yes, and a big syringe besides. They put a tub of water on top of the cow's shed, run their tubes down and up, and made an arrangement that drew every boy in the neighborhood to watch it all the afternoon. It filled the back-yard with slippery pools, before Bridget discovered them. She knew I was not very well, so she did not tell me until to-day. Sometimes, girls, I think I cannot endure such things. I am not what I once was." And the dear old lady sighed, as if the time had been when she could see stomach-pumps destroyed with equanimity. "I wish you would punish Jack," she added: "he richly deserves it."

"I will, whenever you say do it," said Marion cheerfully. If ever Jack was punished, it was when Granty did not know it; for his first squeal called forth from her unconditional pardon, if not a present. Nevertheless, she daily threatened him with the terrors of the law in a way that seemed to her very effective.

"Hester will take her death of cold in that barn. I wish she would come in, and let the old horse alone! She is just like her uncle."

"Yes, Granty. Don't you think, if Hester had been a man, she would have been a doctor?" asked Marion.

"I have not the least doubt of it. She is better fitted for that than for any thing else in the world," said the old lady emphatically. "Now, Dorothy, be kind enough to hand me my glasses and the Bible, and a teaspoonful of Jamaica ginger. I am chilled through. I stopped a while to see if the cow was protected."

Marion reported to Hester Dorothy's suggestion that Granty be approached by some one outside the family, and that with unusual tact.

"By Mr. Severn," said Marion, "in case he approves of the course you have resolved to take. I wonder if he will, and what men like Mr. Craig will say."

"What any one thinks outside of our own family is not to come into consideration," said Hester frigidly, "Dr. Willard's opinion alone excepted. But I do not want Granty to see it in any unpleasant light. I trust you to prevent that."

Had Marion not agreed to talk with Mr. Severn, she would have left it to Dorothy; but when, later in the day, he came for a book to the library, and found her alone, she mentally resolved to have it over with. It was a delightful peculiarity of Marion's, that, when she had any thing to say, she said it without long preludes; not at all with ungraceful abruptness, but clearly and exhaustively. To-day, when Mr. Severn, after talking a while, might have gone away, she drew out the easiest chair for him, saying, "Wait a little longer: I want to tell you something surprising."

She began by talking, more fully than ever before, of her uncle Jack, of Hester's training, tastes, and peculiarities. She touched on their present circumstances lightly, but doing it without false pride, that he might see all the reasons why a lucrative profession would be better than any uncertain means of support. She finally told him Hester's plan, and asked him frankly for his opinion. He had listened, with his face shaded by his hand, hearing her through without an interruption. When he spoke, his friendly tones assured her that his answer would not be a shallow or a prejudiced one.

"I am so glad," he said, "that you did not begin by putting me through a catechism on the 'woman question' in the abstract. If you are a so-called advanced thinker, you might be angry at my conservatism. If you hold too narrow opinions of what a woman can and may do, you would find me a radical, perhaps. The fact is, I have never thought myself wise enough to settle the affairs of all women, and should, in most cases, be puzzled to tell even one woman what Providence intended she should do with herself. If a young lady in my particular parish should appear to me some day, asking my opinion on her studying medicine, she would not get it. I should give her a few general principles of thought, and let her decisions severely alone. You certainly surprise me with this sudden resolution which your sister has taken; but the plan itself is not so surprising. It is perfectly natural that it should have been suggested to her. I have known her only a few months; but I can see that she is admirably fitted for the life she thinks of undertaking. She would put all heart, interest, and enthusiasm into it. She is sensitive, but not at all nervous; has physical courage and perfect health, knowledge of human nature; and she knows when to talk and when to keep still. Every thing else is in her favor. In many respects she would stand, at the outset, on a plane only attained by another after many efforts. I am persuaded it is well that some women should be physicians. I am quite sure your sister would make a good one,—one of the best. Now, you cannot accuse me of giving you an ambiguous answer."

"I am thankful for it," said Marion. "Not that Hester distrusts her own judgment, or that any one's likes or dislikes would have much weight after she had Dr. Willard's professional opinion and the approval of the family; but I wanted to know if it seemed as feasible a plan to you as it did to us. And then," laughed Marion, hesitating a little, "I wanted to use you as a sort of herald to prepare Granty. We want to lay the matter before her most successfully. Could you not turn the conversation in this direction some time, and prepare her to see the plan in a favorable light, if we tell her later what Hester wants to do? Granty is afraid of us sometimes. She thinks that uncle Jack gave us such liberty of thought that we are capable of erratic action. She cannot see we are none of us so young as to be suspected of giddiness and immaturity. She could scarcely be more exercised over a house full of young girls."

The utter absence of affectation in Marion's words

would have made a compliment to their apparent youthfulness silly; and the minister was the last man to be seizing little hooks whereon to hang flattering speeches. Nevertheless, he thought to himself that Miss Marion was much too young to talk in the calmly comical way she did, as if they were a household of quite ancient maidens. In society they were all known as young ladies. Mr. Severn had fallen into this line of thought, forgetting the request just proffered, until Marion's expectant face recalled it to his mind, and he promised to do his best that very evening. Mr. Severn and Granty were excellent friends. She had, from her early years, been a constant reader of the best books; and what she read she did assuredly inwardly digest. At first it was a mystery to him how a nervous little body who talked so irrelevantly of the horse, the dog, and the family, could, five minutes later, give him in forcible language her own thoughtful review of some new book, the title of which he would scarcely have expected her to know. After a while, it was a common thing for him to come where she sat knitting, drop into a chair, and read her a page of a book, or a bit of his sermon perhaps, waiting to hear her terse comments. He told her his congregation owed to her some of the best points in his discourses.

On the evening of this day that Marion talked

with him, he sought the old lady's company, and found her with Dorothy in the parlor. It was always easy to turn the conversation to uncle Jack: so, before long, Granty was telling of his early practice, of days when he rode thirty miles on horseback, carrying his saddle-bags. Mr. Severn drew her on into a most social mood before he said, —

"It seems something to regret that he left no son or nephew old enough to take his practice here in Merriton."

"Yes, indeed! If Hester, now, had only been a man! She is like her uncle, with a little more push and spirit perhaps," said Granty, "but enough like him to make the same sort of a doctor."

"Hester had better study medicine," suggested Mr. Severn blandly.

"What! and go about on horseback with saddle-bags?" ejaculated Granty, as if there were no other way to enter on the career than this, the most primitive.

Mr. Severn smiled as at a jest, and asked her what she thought of women as doctors. She had thought nothing about them, but an hour later she had quite decided opinions. She had agreed with Mr. Severn, that, in this progressive age, what any woman could do well it was to be expected that she would do, even if it were to set broken bones, and administer drugs. However, when Hester's plan was laid before her, she treated it as child's play, and continued so to do until they received a letter from old Dr. Willard, in which the thing was practically discussed and highly recommended. Then they expected from her decided opposition. What she did was to spend one whole day in reflection before she spoke after this fashion: "If you do it at all, do it thoroughly, surgery and all; then you will have two diplomas, one of them in Latin. Your uncle had. Don't get any 'isms' or hobbies, or new-fangled 'pathies.' Promise me one thing, Hester, upon your word and honor!—that you *never* will wear 'bloomers.' I never, never would give my consent to *that* while the world stands. I put my foot on the whole project, unless you bind yourself here on the spot."

Hester gave the promise with all due solemnity; and Granty, taking up her knitting, continued in a plaintive undertone, "Such a thing was never heard of in New England in my younger days! Still Old Mortality would have regular exercise. And there is the strong gig that had a new top just before your uncle died: she could ride around the country in that. It would almost go of its own accord, it knows the roads so well. I would go right at it, Hester, and not bother to take any long course, after all. Tell Dr. Willard you can study up by yourself. Let him tell the college professors you can't spare the time for lectures very well; but you will go on and get your diploma. I don't believe they would press you to come up to all their requirements. — They would, you think, do you?"

Hester laughingly insisted that they would, and explained in detail how she meant to "enter college."

CHAPTER XXI.

Cross-Purposes.

IT was the middle of January, and had been the "greenest" winter ever known in Merriton. But now the snow had been falling softly all night, falling steadily all day for three days, and wonderful was the result. Pete, Jack, and Bridget O'Flarity, had, unitedly, to shovel a path to the barn, where Old Mortality was snugly sheltered. Mr. Severn, when he took his walks abroad, returned to tell of mails delayed, and trains snowed up along the railroads. Granty redoubled her charities, and never sat down to enjoy the warmth of her own fireside without planning to increase the cheer at some dreary one. The third day of the storm the snow ceased falling for a few hours, and the sun came out over all the spotless beauty of the land. About noon Jack rushed through the house to say he had seen a train dragged into town by six engines, and to tell marvellous tales of the passengers' previous adventures. He related it first to Hester, who did not show the lively interest he hoped to excite: so he left her alone in the library, and went to find Granty, who was making mince-pies. A half-hour later some one entered the library; but Hester did not turn, thinking it to be Mr. Severn, who came in and out for books without ceremony.

At the sound of another voice saying, "Miss Hester," she arose, so startled that the color fled from her face for a second.

"Yes. You see me!" exclaimed Mr. Craig. "I came down from the north pole, like a belated Santa Claus, and only hope Jack will be half as glad to see me."

Like a very handsome Santa Claus he looked, with his glowing face and great shaggy coat, only a little under age for that ancient traveller.

"Jack will, and all Jack's friends," said Hester, extending her hand, and gaining color at the pressure it received. "From what place did you come?" she asked. "And was it you who just entered town with six engines?"

"It was, Miss Hester. But do not imagine it took all that steam-power to draw me. There was attraction enough here; but a great deal of resistance had to be overcome. I overcame it, though, and I wish to take it as a good omen. Do you think I may?"

"That depends," said Hester. "Yes, without a

doubt, if you, through life, send six engines ahead of you, every thing will give way to you — or to them."

"You never flatter me; you never encourage me; you are always relentlessly truthful," he returned laughingly, as she invited him to take off the overcoat Miss O'Flarity had given him no chance to remove.

"I started for the West, Tuesday morning. I wanted to stop here and see you; but I had no excuse. The Pepperfields would not take any hint to give me a commission, but fate was more compassionate. The storm delayed me all along the road. I had to pass through Merriton, and I resolved to stop over a day. This same storm is raging West, and I should only run farther into it, if I went on. I do not want to go, having such a good excuse to come and see you."

Hester again assured him that *they* would all be glad to see him (she took the "you" in its plural sense); and then she "feared he was in a famishing condition." No: he had taken a lunch of great magnitude immediately on arriving at the station, and he declared himself in a most calm and contented state of mind and body. Jack appearing just then at the door, after one astonished stare, rushed at the guest, and gave him a rapturous hug, which was quite ardently returned. Mr. Craig owed Jack several good turns, and regarded him as a friend at court. Soon Jack was sent for Miss Marion, who came as smiling and serene as if she were not greatly astonished, and very much confused in her thoughts as to what this visit might signify, if it signified any thing. Hester, after Marion entered, slipped out to tell Granty. She went to the kitchen, where Bridget was ironing, and Granty at a side-table was artistically manipulating pie-crust, of the kind no Irish girl could make; or so said Granty.

Hester went up to the table, and said, "Mr. Craig, the editor of 'The Phœnix,' is in the library. He was on a delayed train, and thought he would stop over a while. His baggage is at the hotel; but we must invite him to dinner, or for longer."

Granty stood with a pie balanced on the palm of her left hand, and her right expressing by gestures the surprise, that, appearing in her countenance, quickly changed there to a look of queer intelligence.

"Humph! He stopped over! I presume he never had another idea after he left Ingleside. Well, it is all right. Dorothy has ordered plenty of poultry. We shall have a nice dinner. Don't put too much sage in the dressing, Bridget: some people do not like it. We are to have company. Miss Marion has a friend come unexpectedly, — a gentleman."

"Mucha, now! but I must have a leetle fun wid

her. Sorry is the chance I ever had before! 'Tis big and purty he is, and a neat way wid him. I let him intil the house, sure!"

"Nonsense, Bridget!" said Granty with dignity, but an amused glance at Hester. "Miss Marion has no time for folly. She could have been settled in life long ago, if she had chosen to marry."

"And who doubts it, thin? There is few good enough for her, and that's thrue!"

Hester was studying the convoluted crust on the pie Granty had in hand. If Mr. Craig had come especially to see Marion, perhaps she had best not call Dorothy at once to go and help entertain him. She turned and went out of the kitchen, meeting Dorothy in the next room. Of course she was asked whose voice it was that sounded out from the library,—a voice as full and deep as Mr. Severn's, only louder.

Hester told her unenthusiastically.

"Is it possible?" exclaimed Dorothy. "Did Marion expect him?"

"No."

"It seems to me he must be rushing things, to leave the city such weather as this."

"Yes, he is rushing things. He came in with six engines," returned Hester coolly.

Both sisters stood a moment on the rug in the

hall, silent, waiting for no especial reason. Hester was taking another look at her own future, — a new outlook, from a strictly personal and feminine standpoint. She was wondering if *her* "day-books," years hence, would count for a life worth as much as another kind of a one, — one that Marion might perhaps live. Under that thought was another and a more bewildering.

Dorothy was reflecting, "I might have known it would come to this — with him. As for Marion, I do not know."

"I will go in there," she said aloud. "We must make him feel at home; and it is awkward for Marion to be left with him at once. If we all know he came to visit her, we must not seem to see it prematurely."

"Of course not: you go in. I will be back soon. I have now to send a letter to Dr. Willard."

"Shall I tell Mr. Craig that you mean to study medicine?"

"It makes no difference," said Hester bravely, — how bravely, neither of them knew.

Before long the sun went under clouds, the snow filled all the air again; but never did a delayed traveller get himself into a snugger nook. Granty would not hear of Mr. Craig's returning to any hotel. As her sister Huldah's friend, she made him welcome with all her own hospitable nature. How many times that day he recalled with secret amusement Marion's letter, that gave him his first perplexing peep into this household! What winsome, cheery women they all were!—unconventional, without pretensions of any sort, yet perfectly at ease, and very entertaining. Their home was also charming: the house and furniture seemed slowly to have come together, by especial laws of fitness. All the books, pictures, quaint rooms, and quainter furnishing, pleased the somewhat fastidious bachelor editor.

At the table he was introduced to Mr. Severn; and each gentleman appeared agreeably impressed by the other. Invited by Marion, Mr. Severn returned to the library with them; and it was a most enjoyable afternoon. Granty afterward declared she had not supposed there was half so much fun and fire in Mr. Severn as there proved to be when he was drawn into conversation with another man his equal in culture. Outside, the storm redoubled its fury; but within, the fires glowed in the deep grates, and Granty, in her best cap, beamed on the company like a benevolent fairy godmother. She talked and listened, knit, and tapped her slipper-toes on the rug; while she fancied she read the thoughts of each one in the circle. There was Mr. Craig. What was more natural for a man of his turn of mind than that he should be attracted by a woman of Marion's? Only he was mistaken in thinking his sentiments reciprocated. He would find this out without any unpleasant explanations, she hoped. Marion could manage that; then they would be excellent friends, just as before. Here was Mr. Severn too. That Hester interested him was plainly to be seen by his remarks the other night and his manner in general. Still, he would acknowledge, that for a minister to take a practising physician for his wife would be the height of absurdity. Dorothy, now, would make either of these men an excellent wife. She wondered if it had occurred to Dorothy herself. She resolved to speak to her about it; to what end, precisely, was not apparent. So Granty pursued her innocent reflections; while the gentlemen's, perhaps, were quite at cross-purposes. Who knows if one of them noted the animation in Marion's dark eyes when excited by conversation, or if the other wondered what Hester thought of, from her seat between the red curtains, when she looked off over the snow-covered fields? It had been Mr. Craig's intention to return to the hotel for the night; but, the storm continuing, Granty insisted that they would be monsters of inhospitality to allow him to go; and he was easily induced to stay. The impression he produced in the house was a very agreeable one. Miss O'Flarity, even, peering at him through a crack in the diningroom door, confided to Pete her opinion that he was of as "fine a figure as any new clothes-pin," and much like to a cousin of hers in Drummonddrusky.

Jack strolled into the office just before his bedtime, and found that Mr. Severn had returned to his sermonizing. He told that gentleman of his first acquaintance with Mr. Craig, and how, in Ingleside, he used "to come almost every night to see us, and now he is the one that writes those letters to aunt Marion in the awful big envelopes. He owns a paper, or a magazine, you know, 'The Old Ghost,' or 'Spook,' or some such queer name."

Something in Mr. Severn's usually serene face caused Jack to think he had spilled ink on his paper. But no: he entirely neglected his writing during the rest of Jack's stay, which was not long. If people were not inclined to be entertaining, Jack's rule was to let them alone. He soon returned to the library, where Mr. Craig and Marion were talking "shop" in a very animated way. It was very pleasing to Marion that there was a topic, in a measure impersonal, on which they could converse with real interest. The cool assumption of every one in the house that Mr. Craig was *her* guest seriously affected her tranquillity. It seemed to her she must be responsible for this impression, yet just how she could not see.

It annoyed her so much, she wished some one would give her a chance to speak on the subject. Some one did. Later, Dorothy asked her if her friend would like a sleigh-ride in the morning, if the weather permitted; and Marion promptly replied that he was aunt Pepperfield's friend.

"Is it possible! But he did not expect to find aunt Pepperfield here, I take it."

Marion went on closing up the house for the night, saying no more. Dorothy left her alone; but Mr. Severn, just then coming through the room, saw her about to open a window and close the shutters. He stopped to do it for her.

"I enjoyed the afternoon with your friend exceedingly," he said. "I have not met a person lately who gave me so much to think over. You must find his acquaintance helpful."

Marion attempted to say that she did, and why, but stammered, hesitated, then blushed so preposterously, that the minister wished he had not embarrassed her, wished he could not read her so easily; most of all, wished that he had not discovered, in a time that was so inopportune, how much he himself possessed of what Herbert Spencer calls the "raw material of human nature,—strong feelings."

The next morning the sky was as blue as turquoise. The sun was dazzling in the splendor it shed over a snow-covered landscape, every angle rounded to spotless beauty, every old hut or barn made pure enough for the abode of fairies, if fairies ever flourish after snow-storms.

Before breakfast, Jack informed Mr. Craig that Granty said, if the roads were at all broken that day, he might enjoy a sleigh-ride, in which case Mr. Severn would go with him. Mr. Craig did not seem to hear. He asked Jack questions about the weather-cock on a neighbor's barn; but soon turning to Hester, who had come in, he said, "You promised me once a drive after a famous trotting-horse, Old Mortality, if ever I came to Merriton. Now I do not insist that you shall hold the reins, or even take out the trotter. You can keep your hands in a muff, and I will select my own fast horse, if you will take the sleigh-ride with me this morning. I have not broken through such great drifts for years. Will you go?"

To say, "Why don't you take Marion?" was impossible. She could only say something to the effect that the drifts would certainly make the sleighing very difficult; but, when they were summoned to breakfast, Mr. Craig spoke of it as a thing to be. After breakfast, he excused himself to go down to the station and ask about trains. Half an hour later he returned in a gay little sleigh with gorgeous robes and a much finer horse than poor Old Mortality. The bells and turnout caused Jack to tumble up erect from a snow-bank at the gate, and then and there administer a hint of full forty-pound power, — a hint which was heroically taken, and heroically given back in this wise: "Jack, I do not want you: there is not room. I want your aunt Hester."

"I could hang on behind."

"You could, but you will not."

While Mr. Craig was arranging the robes to suit his mind, Jack sped into the house, and announced the former's return. This was not necessary. The aunts had seen all from the windows.

"Get your cloak right on, Marion!" cried Granty. "Of course he prefers a lady to Mr. Severn. I was only thinking of their both being men when I proposed they should take Old Mortality."

This fathomless speech was overleaped by Jack, as one would leap a chasm.

"She can't go! He wants nobody but Hester: he told me so! And he said nobody should hang on behind, neither."

His haste to show Marion the futility of any hopes she might indulge as to this last exploit set them all into such a flutter of laughter, that no one betrayed the surprise really felt by each of them except Hester. She calmly waited for Mr. Craig to enter, and say they would go if she was ready, then withdrew to come back soon, dressed for the ride. Granty and Dorothy stood at the window, watching the gay little shell move slowly through the drifts, heard the bells grow fainter and fainter; then they looked inquiringly into space, and, getting no answer therefrom to their unspoken question, they silently departed to see about the dinner. Mr. Severn restrained his desire to look out of the office-window, accused himself of foolish curiosity, but was pleased later to hear Marion's voice afar off in the library. Her being in the house or out need not have affected his sermon; but it certainly did. The mild surprise that permeated the household that morning reached even to the kitchen. Miss O'Flarity, and Miss O'Flarity alone, gave voice to it. She thrust her long neck far out of the kitchen-door to see "Miss Marion and her frind" when they drove away. Seeing, instead, Miss Hester, she exclaimed, "And fut is this thin! It 'ud plaze me to know if he's that bewildered betwixt them he's picked out the wrong won!"

Marion herself, hastily leaving the parlor, went to her own room. Sinking on her couch as gracefully as one of her own heroines, she buried her face in her pillow, and — laughed and laughed until her sides ached with laughter.

Innocent as a guileless, one-idead man may be (all

men are one-ideaed in love), and happy as one who is just where he chooses to be, Mr. Craig chatted pleasantly of various matters, not waiting always for responses to each utterance. He knew Hester too well to expect much mere talk for talk's sake. The road was not at all well broken, and the sleigh moved very slowly; but rapid transit was not the object of this particular ride. It had an object; and in due time Hester found it out.

"I am usually quite bold," he remarked when they were away from the town; "but I am afraid of you, Miss Hester. Yesterday I was even afraid to tell you all the truth when I said I stopped to see you. It was no *after-thought*, I assure you. I started from home with one purpose, and that was to see you. I am going West; but that is nothing. I may surprise you now: you never gave me any chance to show you gradually what I mean to tell you plainly to-day, — that I have loved you ever since — well, perhaps since the day you strolled off among the lunatics, and I found you on the way to the Tombs. If you were not yourself the most sincere and straight-forward woman whom I have ever known, I should fear you might think me impertinent when I say I have dared to hope you knew I loved you, even if I have not courted you. I never tried to hide my interest in you."

They were gliding softly through the great billowy drifts, but so noiselessly that had Hester murmured a word he would have heard her. She was as motionless, as white, as if frozen. He bent forward, determined to make her look up, and asked simply, "Will you be my wife, Hester?"

She raised her eyes, but not at first to his face, only looked out over the limitless snow-fields, seeing nothing. There came into her face an expression uncle Jack's patients had known in his, — the yearning tenderness of eyes that guided the surgeon's unflinching hand. Hester being a woman, her lips trembled when she answered, "I cannot — I could not be that."

"Why not? Would it be impossible to love me, Hester?"

"No: that is not it," she returned, scarcely knowing what she implied. But he interrupted, —

"If you ever could, I can wait. I expected to wait. I was not vain enough to think you could be won without an effort. You do not know me yet, — the best of me, perhaps, as the woman I love better than all the world might know me. It is" —

"No, I do not mean that, either," said Hester in a low tone, but each syllable intensely distinct through earnestness. "I know you better than you imagine. If I could marry any one, I would marry you. I believe now I knew that you did love me. I could not admit it to myself before, because I thought you ought to prefer a very different woman. Everybody would say that : I do myself. I "—

This was a masterful man, by habit seizing the main issue at once; and he knew the woman at his side was not unlike him in this. He looked in her face with will and emotion enough to get out all truth at once, asking, "First, before any thing, tell me this, *Could* you love me? Do you care for my love now at all?"

A fearless light illumined the face turned fully toward him, then a flood of color that retreated as quickly, because the light was wholly of love, not at all of joy. Hester said, "Yes. But you must let me tell you all the rest; and it makes this of no effect."

"This makes all the rest of no effect with me," put in the will of the man, who folded her into the fur robes with his arms, as closely as if taking instant possession; not quite daring to kiss her, near as her face was; chagrined that he did not, when it was too late.

"It does and will," said Hester firmly. "When I tell you all I have to tell, you will see it is impossible that I should marry you."

"There is no such word for me," murmured Mr.

Craig, a shadow creeping over his face, however, at sight of the utter lack of flutter and hesitancy about the outwardly cool young woman.

"Things may not seem to you at all as they seem to me; but I must tell you from the beginning," began Hester. "Our home has always been as you see it now, since I was a little child, only that uncle Jack was there. You never knew him (there will be the difficulty of making you understand);" and Hester's voice faltered as if she were suddenly aware of trying to paint a picture on air, — her background gone.

"Perhaps I imagine your uncle better than you think. Your sister Marion made me feel as if I had known him in life."

"He was father and mother and friend, playmate, teacher, helper, and physician — all in one — to us. He made our lives good, happy, and helpful. As I look back, I only think of him as living for and in other people, — any and all who needed him. I think he would have been miserable, if he had thought one of his family could any time in life shake free from the rest in the way of affection, help, sympathy, of giving herself. Yet he made us very independent, perhaps too much so " —

Hester stopped. How could she ever bring this whole tissue of her past, out of which she had started to weave threads for her future, under the comprehension of a practical man like Mr. Craig? A thousand strands came in to make it up. To him it would all be one strong barrier band on which to try his strength and to test her endurance. While uncle Jack's memory was the power that now nerved her, it yet gave her, along with courage, a creeping loneliness. Something of this, suggesting itself in her face, moved her companion to sympathy; and an instinct told her she must hasten, if she would have that sympathy on his part undemonstrative.

She went on in a voice as unhesitating as a bell in the clear, pulseless air. "It was as a doctor — as 'the doctor' — that everybody loved him, and felt uncle Jack's power. You can see how *real* the man himself must have been, when I tell you that I, studying him with a child's keen eyes and heart, and so on up to full age, — that I have come to think his is the *one* profession, the first and last, capable of being the best. It does wholly with life and with death, — the only two realities; and it is a low conception of the profession that allies it to the body alone. More than a minister's even, — (and what do you think of that heresy?) more than a minister's, I believe it has to do with men's souls; for every soul is in a body, and he who knows nothing of the one cannot know well the other. Think of it! The minister touches the lives of a community — how? He stands above them weekly, and tells them collectively truth they may or may not take to themselves. He lays his hands on their children, marries their young people, prays over their dead. If he is a good fellow-man as well as a good priest, he becomes a confessor, as the doctor is. That is well. When I think how uncle Jack entered into the lives of men and women, it fills me with awe. He carried into his grave, and back to God, secrets that only God knew. I do not think any one outside of a doctor's family can believe how people come to a good, tender-hearted doctor, as (I say it in all reverence) they must have come to Christ the Lord, — silently coming, you know, to bring their helpless or their sore-vexed, the wickedest of them being able to endure his eyes because of his pity."

Hester's voice was stopped as with tears; but her eyes were undimmed, kindling with an enthusiasm that stirred her friend, knowing, as he did, that it was awakened, not by fancy, but by knowledge.

"Yes, Hester," he answered quietly: "you are quite right. But tell me, what has this to do with, or rather what can it have against, our love for one another?"

She shrank back for a second, then answered, — the tremor gone out of her voice, the clearness there again, — "I am going to take up uncle Jack's work where he dropped it. I am a woman; but some women could do it. I can."

"I do not think I understand you. I will when you tell me just what and all you mean," said Mr. Craig slowly, trying successfully to keep all surprise out of his tone, and taking her gloved hand close in his, with an undefined suggestion of holding fast to *his* ideas while they would guilelessly discuss these other matters.

"It takes in so much!" Hester went on, letting her hand alone: there was work enough for it hereafter, when she had done forever with this man she loved. "Long ago I knew I had not only a love of, but a fitness for, uncle Jack's work. He said it: scores of others acknowledged it. When he died he left us little more than a home. There are five of us. He told us before he died to cling together: by that, of course, he meant mutually care for and help one another. It will cost more each year to keep the home comfortable, and educate Jack. We must be quite self-supporting, of course. I am going to study medicine, and here, among uncle Jack's friends, practise his profession. Now you see why I cannot be your wife."

Surprise, doubt, fear, had clouded Mr. Craig's face by turns; but when, at Hester's last word, the color rushed over her face, he exclaimed, "That was brave in you when you stood all alone! I honor you for it. But it is a man's work, after all: I mean, darling, it is hard, relentless work; and a woman ought to be cared for as I will care for you. The rest will be so easily adjusted, Hester. If I were a poor man, there might be a hindrance; but I am rich, and what I have we will share. Do you think those whom you love I should not love also? And when I am in the family, one of you, does it make any difference as to whether a brother or a sister dispenses the money? It shall be a *sister*. I will settle on you a yearly income larger than dear old uncle Jack's could have been. We will educate little Jack for the family doctor."

"He never would make one in the world: it is not in him. But it is in me. No. If it were just the money question, I — that involves what all the rest would wish"—

"Leave it to me, Hester. If they say I may have you, will you come? Will you stay *here?*"

That time, certainly, he would have kissed her, if she had staid *there;* but she recovered as erect a position as ever a person knowing her own mind could, and said, "It is too late now. I have decided for all time. I can do this thing better than I can do any other work under the sun; and do it I must."

They were driving along in a reckless fashion, not as regards speed, for the horse could hardly flounder through the drifts, — quite reckless as to route; for Hester, derelict as a guide, was letting him graze stone walls, and do every thing but climb trees; which last, indeed, was about the only feat horse and driver did not attempt. On they went. Hester, now that all was over, was conscious of cold and weariness, was wishful for home. But she mistook the spirit of this man. He carefully re-arranged the robes, gathered up the reins, and said cheerily, " Well, my dear friend, then I say, 'Study medicine, graduate, be a doctor.' Only it puzzles me a little to know how people hereafter will know that I am an editor when you are Mrs. Dr. Craig. I shall get credit for being the titled partner; but I shall not care, if you are not jealous."

"You are very good and true. I can never be sorry I have known you. I thought that most men were scornful on such points. I thought, too, that you might be," said Hester with honest pleasure. "No man ought to marry a woman who is a doctor, for his own comfort; and no unselfish woman would make a victim of him. But I like to have you say this, and know you are willing to do it, even for a moment."

"Not at all for a moment: I shall marry you for all time."

"No, Mr. Craig. I know and you know that when you go home, and think it all out calmly, you will see that for me to adhere to my determination will make it wise and best for me to remain unmarried. As I am situated, I need have no domestic cares. I shall, by work outside the home, make up to those within it what they do for me. We shall be mutually independent and dependent. This is what a woman can seldom do. And it would not be true if I were to marry, and separate myself from my present home. I know exactly what I have undertaken. I am not a visionary girl, running wild with new ideas of a mission. I have planned a life full of work; but I am strong. I can see the end from the beginning; and I think it is not an unworthy life for me, or a selfish one. In detail, I propose to do just this."

Hester, then, in few words, told all there was to tell, while the man who loved her listened in silence, — listened and reasoned, and tried to find out what manner of woman this was. He had not understood her, after all. One thing was clear: she was womanly to the core. He had few weapons to disarm her, and he knew it, — nothing but his love; and how much of a power that was he could not yet tell. If she had only taken up some plan of life that he could by argument make distasteful, could prove that she did not know all it involved; if he could show her unfitness for such a life — he could do none of these things. He admitted with a secret regret her peculiar fitness for the work. Insight, skill, strength, tenderness, — she possessed them all.

When she had ended, he answered, "If much you have said did not come to me as true, I would be glad; for I am selfish. I want you to myself and for myself; but I am not blind or a bigot. I confess I think you might do all this, and do it nobly. If you must, you must."

"*Yes, I must.*"

"Then I shall not ask you to give it up: you would only think the less of me for so doing. Will you answer me one more question?"

"Yes, any question."

"Do you think a woman who for love marries a man who means to be worthy of her, and lives the best life she can, helping him to do the same — do you think she has a life less noble than that you mark out for yourself? Will you be as happy all alone?"

For the first time great tears filled the woman's eyes, and he was almost (but yet not quite) sorry he so pressed her.

"I was not choosing between the two lives when I decided. I think almost all women are happier well married than single. But every thing without and within me has turned me in this way I have marked out. I know I was not vain or ambitious in deciding I wanted to be a helper: I knew I could be. And if I am alone in one sense — well, uncle Jack was; but people loved him to make up for it. You should have known how they showed it when he died!"

"You will be loved, Hester, and you must be a helper, wherever you are. God makes such women as you for that. But we *must* unite these two lives, and have you live them both. We can, or we must try, impossible as it seems to you."

"Oh, you don't know me at all!" cried Hester with a change of tone almost comical. "I cannot come within rules. I am not at all tractable. You could do nothing with me anyway: you would be heartily tired if you tried."

"No, no!" laughed Mr. Craig. "Don't you know the delight of an editor's heart is the most original article he can find? What we will do is just this " —

What they did was to awake to the fact that the horse was meandering into somebody's orchard, and entangling his legs in a rail fence. The fence maintained its position: the horse sank slowly out of sight. The sleigh capsized. Hester, snugly enveloped in the robes, rolled gently off in one direction; and the editor of "The Phœnix" found himself projected into the limbs of a scraggly apple-tree, like a large and most unseasonable bird. He floundered as speedily as possible toward Hester; but, before he reached her, she was spreading the robe over the snow in a way to walk upon it, while she called his prompt attention to righting the sleigh, and helping the horse. Fortunately nothing was broken, and the accident served a good purpose, in that it suggested to them that they had better turn around. It would be useless to repeat in detail all the subsequent conversation. What had been already said by each was said again in other words; but neither was convinced by any new argument. Hester refused to reconsider her decision. She would not be persuaded into a conditional engagement.

"It would only result in trouble for each of us," she said, "and would all along make it harder for me. I cannot do any thing half way. If I am to study in these coming months, my mind must be undistracted."

A narrower-minded man would have been irritated by opposition, or would have given her up at once as too strong-willed. When there seemed no plea that Mr. Craig could urge, he gathered up the reins resolutely, and exclaimed, "You will not promise to marry me; but I have one comfort, you will not marry any one else, — that is, I hope not?"

Hester promptly answered, "No."

"Well, then, I shall wait. Physicians retire sometimes from practice. Fifty years from now, you may be at leisure. I will leave my duties as managing editor, and run down here for you; that is, if I cannot do it sooner. Hester, remember it took six engines to overcome the obstacles that separated me from you yesterday; but I found you. I am going home to order an engagement-ring engraved with six puffing boilers. There is a beautiful suggestion of success to me in the emblem, and I believe I shall use the ring."

He glanced at Hester; but she made no answer. She had said all she had to say. He knew now, as well as if told, that henceforth she would be his shy, noncommittal friend, nothing more. He stopped the horse with a sudden impulse, and they sat motionless in a silent, snow-white world, not a human habitation in sight.

"Hester, is it simple truth that you would marry me if you did not believe that either your husband or your work would be less to you than was wise?"

"Yes."

"Will you promise me, that if I am going to die, and send to you, you will come and be my doctor, while you can give that your undivided attention, then, when I am really going, and cannot interfere with further professional duties, you will *marry me?*"

She thought he was ridiculing her; and the look she gave him was a revelation of the spirit of a "shy, cool" woman under provocation. He met the look with one that outlasted hers, and quenched it; then he said, "If I am going to die, Hester, will you be my wife? It will be not much to ask at the last, after refusing me happiness for all my life."

She answered, "Yes;" and they went the rest of the way almost in silence.

Nobody at the cheerful dinner-table would have imagined, from the collected, gentle demeanor of their guest, how stirring to his emotional nature had been the morning sleigh-ride. Hester was impenetrable, or would have been, had any one undertaken to study her. Jack announced that the railroad track was clear, and trains were running. Mr. Craig made known his intention to proceed on his journey that afternoon, and in consequence spoke repeatedly of the pleasure he had received from visiting them all in their own home. Before going, he arranged with Marion for a series of articles of a sort she felt a renewed interest in undertaking, and which were sure to prove profitable. Then, with hearty handshakes, with a hug from Jack, a message left for Mr. Severn, and many taken to the Pepperfields, the editor of "The Phœnix" was gone.

"I forgot," said Granty, when the echo of his voice had died away, "to ask him if he was a New-England man. I presume he was originally. — Do you know, Marion?"

Marion had gone with Jack to see his snow fort.

"Oh! — Hester, it is you, is it? Well, he is a very fascinating gentleman, isn't he? Did you notice any thing queer about the gravy this noon? Bridget put curry-powder into it. She declared she had seen it done, and it was nice. I don't exactly see what he came for. I suppose Marion would not tell, if she knew. Queer, his taking you to ride, if he is particularly interested in her. I myself do not like quite so much *finesse* in such matters. But dearie me! what does it matter?"

Hester did not hear her. She was wondering if she should consider herself a fool, a genuine woman, or a possible power, — perhaps somewhat of all. Should she go away and think the matter over in a feminine way? Perish the thought! There was danger there. She went instead to the barn, and sought out Pete's shortcomings, and meted out justice to him. She came in again, and read a lecture on anatomy. She was cast down, but not destroyed.

CHAPTER XXII.

Two Years Later. Dorothy to Hester.

MARCH 9, 18–.

DEAR HESTER, — "Time in its ever-onward course" (as Parson Welles's anniversary sermons always began) "has brought us once more" to the day when a letter must be written you. Granty will not let the duty be omitted, although I believe you would not know the difference, absorbed as you are with your dreadful "goings-on." Aunt Huldah wrote to Granty how you went to hospital clinics with students from the college, and sat upright through some operation at which a certain young *man* fainted. What a perfect fossil you must have become! Or do you pride yourself on your nerve? I suppose it is that. Granty tells vague but blood-curdling stories of medical students to Bridget; and Bridget says if ever she knows of Miss Hester's "cutting up a Christian after she gets home," she will "lave widout a word o' warnin'." Aunt Huldah says Mr. Pepperfield is very much out of health: we are all so sorry to hear it! Don't you know enough yet to help him? I suppose you are greatly pleased to be chosen valedictorian. I often wonder what uncle Jack would say to your success so far. Granty is well, and busy as usual. She has been elected president of the Ladies' Missionary Society. It would please you to hear the artless way in which she tells the members their duty, and her righteous indignation when they do as they please. Jack is taking a course of Jules Verne. We shall never have him again until after he has been to the moon, sounded the sea, dwelt in coral caves, and swept the universe on the tail of a comet. He talks in his sleep about mysterious islands and unknown beings with singular titles. When not reading, he is at his inventions. He told me last night of a plan to supply pure air to steerage passengers in steamships. By the same means, the ships could be made to float after any accident, and, in case of fire, this surplus air could be used as an extinguisher. Who knows but that he may make us rich some day? Why do you never speak of Mr. Craig? Aunt Huldah says he boards with her: so you must see him, at least at the table. I suppose you study evenings. Well, we are glad you get your diploma in a few weeks.

We have had the office repainted, but have not changed any familiar object. The big red chair would look fresher with the arms varnished; but we left it worn as it used to be. We also left the three old doctors' portraits over the desk, with the gilt pestle and mortar behind. Do you remember when it was the sign on a pole by the front-gate? We have added a few touches here and there, put new curtains on rods, a new table-cover, easy-chairs, and a paper-rack. I trained a long ivy to cover the tarnished frame of that old chap who discovered the circulation of the blood. And, oh! now I propose to tell you something that will quicken the circulation of your blood, unless your wits have been sharper than ours. *Marion is engaged to be married!*

Granty has always believed there was something behind Marion's long correspondence with Mr. Craig; but it must always have been business, after all. Of course, now you know it is Mr. Severn; for, as Marion naively asks, "Who else is there" to whom she could be engaged?

We found it out in this way. One night last week there was a merry-making at the Scudder farm. Have I told you that Mrs. Molly has *two* beautiful babies, twins? Mr. Scudder is as delighted as if his home-circle did not already resemble a juvenile boarding-school. They (the twins) being now five months old, he conceived the idea of having a great christening party, and we were, of course, invited. All was done in fine style: his mother-in-law took care of that. Moreover, there was a whole-souled hospitality about the affair that is lacking sometimes in her own parties. Mr. Scudder's outer man is quite transformed. He looks and appears well. It was a beautiful moonlight night, and Granty and I rode over in the phaeton. Mr. Severn had a carriage, and asked Marion to go with him. Old Mortality was in one of his moods. He crawled along, and I thought the twins would be celebrating some other episode in their lives by the time we got there, — their majority perhaps. Mr. Severn, on the contrary, had a fast horse, and went the "short cut," which we did not take, as Granty thinks the hill dangerous. I was surprised, when we drove in at the Scudder gate, to see Mr. Severn draw quietly up *behind us*. I said, " Did you have any accident?"

Marion did not speak; but Mr. Severn tried to turn it off by one of his absurd Shakspearean quotations. He remarked, "Sweet flowers are slow, and weeds make haste."

"Dear me!" I returned, "is that what ails you? I did not think of you two as being in what he calls your 'salad days,' when you are 'green in judgment.'"

They were in such a happy frame, they seemed to find that especially funny, and the truth flashed upon me. Granty could not be gotten into the house until she told him his horse must be all fagged out from previous hard driving, and that we could take Marion home, so he would have a lighter load. When we were in the dressing-room, I said to Marion, "What have you to say for yourself? Is it so, or is it not? and, as Granty would say, how long has this been going on?"

She laughed; she blushed; she said, "Let us quote Shakspeare once all around. 'Fortune brings in some boats that are not steered.' I did not know where I was drifting when it began; but *now I do*."

We went then to the parlor, and greeted Mrs. and Mr. Scudder, the Howells, and innumerable youthful Scudders, all resembling more or less "she that was," until by and by the twins, belonging to "she that is," were brought in, and Mr. Severn christened them. His face was radiant with joy over that scene (or some other); and he never winced while the two wailed, and gnashed their gums, at being called Edwin Theodore and Theodora Edwina. He got the final "a" on to the girl with the blue ribbon, too, and not on to the boy with the red label as I feared he would.

Mr. Severn says he has been in love with Marion for nearly three years, but until lately he supposed she was engaged to Mr. Craig. Does not that prove there must have been something in our fancies? Marion is very undemonstrative. She says she loves him, and intends to marry him. Think of that for point-blankedness in one who devotes her time to showing how other women expatiate over their emotions; how they weep, blush, tremble, and experience new and thrilling what-you-may-call-'em's! It does not seem proper for her merely to say she is happy, and have done with it. Granty is very much pleased. Marion will marry goodness, culture, some money, above all, a New-England person. This is a high-toned proceeding, according to her ideas. You must know, Hester, that, away down in Granty's heart, she thinks of *your* doings as startling, brilliant, perhaps commendable, but not what any of her aunt Leggett's family ever desired, and which all her other ancestors happily died without the sight of. You will be interested to know that we have gotten rid of all your hens. They were in some respects rather ornamental; but they never laid any eggs, and were the toughest creatures to eat you can imagine. Pete and Jack had built an elegant villa for them; but, once let out, they never would go home until morning, but would roost up in the plum-trees, half buried in the snow. Nightly Pete had to grapple with them, or leave them there to freeze. They scratched and pecked him, of course. He or they had to be sacrificed. Marion and I could not endure it. Their society was nothing to the vexation they caused: so we have cooked them two by two.

Marion says you dislike ministers, and you will be savage with her, she fears. Now, don't be rude, Hester: there is no use in it. Tell aunt Pepperfield we will write all the plans when they have matured them. Marion expects to stay right along here with us after they marry. Now I must end my letter. Jack sends love.

Yours,
Dorothy Prescott.

On finishing this letter, Hester searched her desk to find a certain letter from which she made extracts. It gave her a purely feminine satisfaction to put at the end of the very kind and sisterly letter she immediately wrote to Marion a paragraph like this:—

"What makes you imagine that I do not like ministers? 'I think Mr. Severn a very harmless sort of a person,' and I do not agree with a well-known authoress who once said, 'How can a woman be deluded enough to marry a minister, no matter how good he is? If he is puffed up by conceit and spiritual arrogance, as many of them are, what does she do? How terribly bored an intelligent woman must be by having always to listen to her own husband's sermons; to have him preach her in sentences she could finish for him, if he choked midway! The idea is dreadful! Minister's wives — poor wretches!' &c. The woman that wrote that, Marion, must have been prejudiced in some way. Don't you think she was?" . . .

CHAPTER XXIII.

Granty to Aunt Pepperfield.

(Twelve months later.)

DEAR SISTER, — I have been trying all the week to get a chance to write to you; but more or less of the care of this great house rests on me. The girls do pretty well; but young people cannot have the judgment of older ones, let them do their best. Huldah, I cannot realize that poor Mr. Pepperfield has gone. He had been ill so long, it need not have surprised us so much at the last; but still it was a great shock. We think you are very wise in your decision to break up housekeeping, and we are so glad to think of having you back as one of us for all time to come! Why, Huldah, I did not think Mr. Pepperfield was a rich man. I never thought any thing much about it, beyond the fact of your having enough. I am very glad now to learn that you are left in such easy circumstances. Money is a matter of very little importance in this world, anyway, so long as one has food, raiment, and enough for other reasonable demands. I have had sometimes to reprove the girls for undue worry about making "ends meet," as Dorothy says. What if they don't meet? I tell her the Lord will fill up the gap with something. He always has, and it ill becomes us to doubt him. Dorothy is like the New-Testament Martha. But I started to say that you would be just as welcome back, if you should return as you went, — with only yourself and your trunk: so I do not hesitate to add that we are glad you are rich, comparatively speaking. Why should you not cast in your lot with us? For whom should we two old people live, if not for these children of our sister? Perhaps you had better bring your best furniture, as you suggest. I like a change once in a while; and ours begins to show service. Can you not select some of the finest plants from yours also? and don't sell off any of those pretty Chinese curiosities you showed me once. You have not seen Marion's husband yet, have you? His mother was one of the old Winchesters. I heard of them in my younger days. He is a very kind, thoughtful man, so careful for my comfort, that it seems as if he must always have been in the family. You are glad, I know, to hear often of Hester's remarkable success in her practice. She has all her uncle's old families in the village and country. The sign over the door of the office was never taken down; and "Dr. Prescott" does now for her. His old patients come morning, noon, and night, exactly as they used to come; and, when Old Mortality trots up to the door, I often expect to see the dear old man appear, instead of Hester. I say Old Mortality *trots*, which may surprise you. There is something very queer in this. You know, before our brother died, he said this was a good, strong horse, and we had better keep him. We did; but he never appeared to feel well — except his appetite. We tried every thing for feed, thinking that made the difference. He had mixtures and plain food, oats, clover, Timothy, Indian meal, buckwheat, stale bread, carrots, swill, stuff called broads — no, shorts, and I don't know what else unless it was sawdust. We consulted the neighbors, because sometimes he was swelled up like a beer-barrel, and did not travel any faster. Sometimes he grew *minching*, and looked weak, and so pitiable, that we let him stand still in the stable.

When Hester came home, she took him in charge, as if he were a patient demoralized by quacks. She examined his teeth, and looked him well over to see if he was worth training; then she put him on proper (as she said) feed for a month, and got him to look splendid. I was sorry to have her buy a whip with a lash long and very snappy; but she did. You know young doctors are always hard on horses. Her uncle, good man as he was, used up several in his day: he would not go slow. Well, Hester started one day, with Old Mortality, and off he paced more deliberate than ever. I saw the new whip coming out, and I shut my eyes, until I heard Mr. Severn laughing immoderately. I just caught one glimpse of the horse and Hester going over the hill like — I don't know what. Mr. Severn said Old Mortality rolled up his eyes in surprise, waited until the whip sung through the air a second time, then he went like the wind. He has gone so ever since — for Hester. When I go, he steps along about as usual. I let him. Poor fellow, he has his failings; but so have we all, if we are not horses. Yes, Hester has all the first families; and Dorothy says she might get rich, and have a very easy time, if she would insist on regular office-hours, and choose her own patients. You might as well talk to the north star. She goes where she likes and when she sees fit. If nothing much ails Mrs. Judge Pinkham, — who wants her to coddle her up, no matter what she charges, — instead, as she says, of "dancing attendance" on her, she will leave her fussing, and ride six miles or more to attend to some poor little pauper, who had much better staid out of the world, — to my thinking. That is brother Jack over again. He doctored the rich because they needed him, and the poor for the very same reason. Time and again I used to think of a verse in the Bible, though there was no real connection of ideas. It was with her uncle Jack as with David: "Every one that was in distress, or every one that was in debt, or every one that was bitter of soul" (as the margin reads) "gathered themselves unto him." But, dearie me! to come down to the point, he was only doing right; and I never want Hester to refuse any help that she can give. I suppose, from what you say, that you will not break up housekeeping until May. That is about six weeks from now. Would you like Dorothy to come and help you? I shall have the south rooms made ready for you here: you like those best, I believe. There! I must see if Bridget has made a pudding for dinner. All send love. Take care of yourself, and do not get sick. It is very sad for you to be breaking up your pleasant home in Ingleside; but this is a world of change. Mr. Pepperfield was one of the kindest of men, and one to be greatly missed. Those antique brass candlesticks you had in your east room please bring. I admire them very much. I hope the Lord will keep you in peace and safety until we meet.

Your Affectionate Sister.

P.S. — Mr. Severn and Marion talk of going to Europe next summer. Did I tell you how well her new book is selling? Mr. Craig wrote her he was delighted with it, and sent her a quantity of press commendations.

CHAPTER XXIV.

The Last of Hester Prescott.

> "If I do vow a friendship, I'll perform it
> To the last article." —SHAKSPEARE.

ONE day early in April, Hester took the express-train for Ingleside under circumstances most peculiar, and in the frame of mind of one awakened from a sound sleep, who tries to remember where he was when last conscious, where his head is now, and if he is not mistaken about having awakened at all. A few hours before, she had been riding placidly along a country lane, with Jack as driver, stopping to let him scurry into the near woods, and pick wake-robins, while she thought what next to do for old Mrs. Blake's unruly liver. They were driving in at the home gate a little later, when Pete rushed at her with a telegraphic message, the three lines of which had made all her mental operations go on after the manner of a kaleidoscope, — changing every moment; the whole tissue of her thoughts made up of strange fragments.

"*Mr. Craig is very ill. He cannot live, and wishes to see you.*"

"What does it mean? What can he want of you?" asked Marion, coming out into the sunshine to know if aunt Pepperfield had sent any message that concerned them all, and taking the paper from Hester, who stood as if paralyzed. It was only for a moment; then she said, "Mr. Craig wanted to marry me a few years ago. I refused him; but I promised, if he were going to die, I would go to him, — would marry him. It means that. Let me go without any more questions. I shall start on the noon-train, but I have work to do first."

When Hester's voice had that ring, people always obeyed, and the most talkative held their peace, even if they did not know why. Marion found a travelling-bag, filled it, did all she could do, and, knowing Hester, she was not surprised to see her, in the time that followed, making out prescriptions, consulting once a medical book, leaving medicine properly labelled for various persons, and finally going to see if a brother-doctor would take charge of her business until she returned. It was, nevertheless, one of the strangest, longest hours in Hester's experience, from the fact that she lived it double in a sense. There was, as it seemed, *one* of her that went right on, by sheer will, with duty and work. Another self was whirled here and there with excitement, busy with memory, with doubt, with love aroused, and the pain of something akin to regret, — for what, she even then did not know; but she did know, as she journeyed on hour after hour that day, what her decision long ago had cost her. She wondered at herself as she might have done at another who possessed character enough to be firm under pressure. With inconsistency, she was not sure she was glad that she had been firm. If the past was bewildering in review, the future in its outlook was — what? A plunge into darkness, a fight alone in the shadows; and then — then there was *work*. In that moment Hester knew she was in earnest, and that she had made no mistake in clinging to that work. While she loved this man to whom she was going so much that she dared to show that love in the presence of the death-angel, and declare it holy enough to stand there, she was also as sure, that, outside that presence, her work would await her, and would not seem, when she took it up again, like something that had lost a glamour. It would be, as it had been, very good, — the thing that it was in her to go on with, because she must.

There are many women who can love one other human being — child, lover, or husband — with a love that is marvellous. There are a few (even fewer women than men) who are drawn to love all other human beings because of their very humanity. Unless death left such a man or woman the last one of the race, he could not make that one wholly miserable. Only to be needed by none would be such a one's misery. But you may be sure few theories of life, few precepts for her future, drew Hester's thoughts long from the man to whom she was going. This awful new suggestion of death was so much worse than mere separation from him, knowing him to be well and prosperous. There was but one other thing that could have pierced her as deeply, — the knowledge of his marriage.

She was conscientious enough to be shocked when she thought of this, because she supposed she had been a better physician to her own malady. So far as he alone was concerned, she did wish him to be happy, by marriage, if need be; but as it concerned her, after all these months it was as it was. This was a revelation that surprised her, a fact that might not have showed its white face on the surface, if such a powerful tumult had not stirred the depths: being there, however, up it came.

Whatever Hester may have thought of her summons, it was evident on her arrival that aunt Pepperfield had no suspicion of there being any thing beyond a mere friendship between Mr. Craig and her niece.

"I did not know whether you would come or not," were her first words. "It seemed a wild notion of his; yet the doctor declared he was perfectly rational: so what could I do but send for you? Perhaps he fancies you may think of some new treatment. There have been several consultations, and I do not suppose there is any hope. Only think of it! Such a man, and just in the prime of life!"

Hester, after a moment, asked, "What ails him? and how long has he been sick?" Then she sat still, and let aunt Huldah take off her hat, and bring her hot coffee, hoping she would get through the sooner her kindly offices, and tell an uninterrupted story. At last her aunt dropped back on to the sofa, where she had passed the night (it was not yet daylight), and, finding Hester impatient to listen, began: —

"You know I expected to be all broken up in my housekeeping by the first of May. Well, three or four weeks ago Mr. Craig, who was looking for a new boarding-place, complained of feeling ill. He did not eat any thing, could not write, finally became much worse. I will say just here that nobody has decided what ails him. He has had as many diseases as he has had doctors to examine him. Each one of them, so it seems to me, has chosen a different organ, and located the trouble there, — all except the regularly attending doctor, and he saves himself by calling it a 'complication.' I have heard it one day explained as a terribly disturbed action of the liver, next day as a mysterious trouble in the stomach, once as dropsy, often as wrong state of the heart, ever so many times as his different *ducts*, whatever they are: I suppose you know all about them. Well, he has grown steadily weaker, does not suffer so much pain; but he loses life out of him each day. We all see that, and he knows it. The doctors say very little now. The old nurse in there says they are afraid to be too explicit, for fear of a *post mortem* examination that might prove they did not know what they were talking about. Dreadful, isn't it?" she exclaimed, seeing Hester shiver.

"Yesterday he asked if it was not time that he attended to any thing left undone (he made his will last week); and the doctor said yes, do any thing he had to do at once. We understood that, as he did, to be an admission that all hope was past. He talked with the doctor a while alone, seemed perfectly calm, but asked that you might be sent for."

Hester had cowered down over the fire rigid and dumb: she now asked in a muffled voice, "When can I see him?"

"Not before ten o'clock this morning, the doctor said: that is his brightest time. He changed his medicine last night, and began a quite new treatment: so he wishes to keep him quiet long enough to see the effect."

Hester asked no more questions. Aunt Huldah went on in the fashion of a good old lady sure of an interested listener, and proceeded with certain criticisms, quite regardless of the fact that Hester's own name was adorned with an "M.D."

"I tell you, Hester, doctors are just as human as ministers; and *they* are about the most human of any creatures going. Such an unsatisfactory, noncommittal set as they are, too, taken together! and what they tell outsiders amounts to saying, that, if the sick man gets well, he will be likely to live. We have had three consultations here. Five or six doctors arrived one day. They went in and took a sort of an inventory of all the damaged stock in the poor man's earthly tabernacle; then they came out and went to the library, where I could hear them, and talked him over. I always supposed he had a splendid constitution; but when they suggested the things that might have ailed him, — away back, you know, 'primal causes,' as they said, of this — this 'complication,' — why, I wondered he ever lived long enough to die this time. And whatever else he had, or did not have, those *ducts* came in. Now, Hester, tell me, have we all got such tricky things? All liable to such disturbances inside of us? and whatever are they for, anyway? They seem so deep in, nobody can reach them. His must be in an awful state, perfectly awful! though how or which one it was the doctors never agreed. Sometimes, when I supposed they were coming at something, they would settle back and ponder. After a long silence one day, the great Dr. Sparks said, 'The chief trouble with Craig is his assimilation. If he could eat a square meal, and keep it where it belonged, he might get well.' Seemed to me I could have said that without graduating at a college, or practising forty years."

Hester sat immovable, possibly hearing, perhaps heeding, nothing. But aunt Huldah must free her mind. Having done so, she exclaimed, "Why, Hester! how dragged-out you do look! Won't you go and lie down until breakfast is ready?"

"I would rather sit here by the fire," said Hester, "where I can hear them moving overhead, and know if any thing happens. You go and lie down."

To her great relief, aunt Huldah went, returning once to say, in a way much like Granty, "I have perfect faith in the doctors, Hester: they stand at the head of their profession."

"Yes, oh, yes!" said Hester wearily. "I know what doctors can do, and what they cannot."

The time went slowly by; but at last the first rays of daylight struggled into the room. The fire burned out; the footsteps above were not as frequent; and, when aunt Huldah re-appeared, Hester had gone to the room assigned her. She came down at breakfast-time looking fresher, in a thinner dress, with her hair smoothed away from her face, which was colorless enough to startle aunt Pepperfield. Moreover, something in the expression of Hester's eyes set her thoughts at work; and it now first occurred to her that there might be something more than mere friendship between Mr. Craig and Hester. She talked less, and went about the house, anxiously awaiting the hour when the doctor should come. When he came, he brought with him a clergyman, — a fact not at all strange in her opinion. She saw them go directly to the sick man's room, where, a little later, Hester was summoned. Into many such rooms had Hester entered in this last year; but never had she carried into one such a heavy heart as she took with her this day.

The bright morning light fell on the bed, and the eager face turned toward her was not as changed as she expected. It was only in the shrunken flesh over the massive frame-work of bone that one saw the ravages of disease. The expression of that face was purely questioning: it hardly needed that he should bring out in syllables, "Will — you — keep the — promise?"

When Hester answered, "Yes," he smiled at her in great contentment, reached out his hand for her to hold while she sat by the bed. The minister stood quietly by the window. The doctor, moving glasses on the table, prepared and gave Mr. Craig a spoonful of something; then aunt Pepperfield was sent for, coming with astonishment written in every line and wrinkle of her goodly countenance. The nurse whispered to Hester. She arose and went to the other side of the bed. Mr. Craig put his trembling right hand in hers. The clergyman came forward; and, in the presence of the witnesses there assembled, he performed the marriage-ceremony, and pronounced Winthrop Craig and Hester man and wife.

Afterwards there was the perfect calm which the doctor insisted upon. Aunt Huldah staid only to see Hester bend over the dying man, and give him the kiss he had waited for; then she fled to a spot where she could weep, as if her heart was breaking, with pity for the woman in there, whose eyes were dry, but had in them a look no tears could take away. She understood every thing now as she could not before; and, when old Dinah sought her out, she poured into her ears the story.

"You know, Dinah, he said to me, after he made his will that day, that he had left all he had to his best friend. He is rich, but he had no near relatives. He did that first, and then wanted this marriage, that Hester might inherit his property. She is so queer, she might have refused to marry if she had known what he meant to do."

When, several hours later, Hester came for some ice, aunt Huldah, whose thoughts were in a fearful turmoil, assailed her with this piece of information. Hester stared at her as if she did not understand; but, standing there waiting for Dinah to bring the ice to her, it dawned upon her that this was *one* reason, perhaps *the* reason, Mr. Craig demanded the promise that far-away day of his brief courtship, — that strange day of snow and whiteness, cold, like all the days since that in any way had been connected with their friendship. If she would not let him, living, care for her, dead, he would guard her life from struggles of one kind, — from all chance of poverty. He showed himself in this. The tears poured down her cheeks. It seemed cruel that within her stirred just then the question, "Could there not have been some way to make your life and his harmonious, if he were so true, so stable, and yet so undemanding?"

There were in the next day no more consultations. The doctor came and went, whispered outside the door with Hester, who had already inspired him with professional respect. The nurse saw half her work taken from her hands by one even better trained than herself; and the patient, — it was enough for him to lift his eyelids and to see his wife, to close them and hold fast to her, as if, the time being short, death alone should separate them.

And now, what more is there to write? The simple facts. Mr. Craig's case was given up as hopeless by five doctors, his wife included. In consultations he was pronounced all wrong, from the crown of his head to the sole of his foot, — outwardly a wreck, inwardly a complication! Worst of all, as aunt Huldah thought, there were those "ducts."

In the face of all this he began to get better, to assimilate (not a "square meal" at once, however), to sleep; and his life came slowly, surely, creeping back. One spring morning the truth was evident: he would get *well*, ducts and all. He began to gaze after Hester, when she left his side, as if he were in heaven, only he knew he was on earth, and wickedly rejoiced that he was likely to be for a while longer. He would laugh silently, smiles running over his pale face, his eyes twinkling with mischief. When Hester was by him, he developed a habit of turning his face into the pillow, and letting go her hand, as if he were ashamed of himself. One day when she was alone with him, he said, looking her in the eyes, "Hester, I am going to get well."

"I know it."

"It seems like an awful fraud." Then he laughed, and she laughed. They were like two ridiculous children, — this editor of "The Phœnix," and this woman with two diplomas, one of them in Latin.

"I did not mean to," he added with real humility, following a paroxysm of levity. "The doctors pronounced me going; and, in the natural course of things, I ought to have gone. I beg your pardon, Mrs. Hester. Now, what are we going to do about it?"

"I am sure I don't know," she returned calmly. "It is time you had your aconite."

He meekly swallowed the dose, and added proudly, "You are *my wife*."

"I know it."

There seemed nothing to be made out of her in that way: so he said, a good deal of vigor going out of his voice, "You will do what you think is best. I can trust you, even if it should be hard, if only you are sure you do right. It would be unmanly to forget the way I gained you."

Hester shook up his pillows, brushed the hair off his forehead, seeing what a handsome one it was. Her lips twitched: she longed to be vicious, to tease him with nonsense. She caught his eye, black with eagerness, and said instead, "Did I not promise — until death?"

"Yes: but you thought it was coming."

"So it is some day. In the mean time I shall not tell lies."

They were very sentimental until Dinah arrived with beef-broth.

"Perhaps there will not be any thing lost, and much gained, in the way things have happened," he ventured later. "At any rate, we can do our best to have it so."

She gave a laugh that made his heart leap, and exclaimed, "Yes. It is only another case of 'complication.' The result may be simple, and is — happy."

While these days slipped away, — and veritable honeymoon days they were, too, — the family at Merriton held not a few unprofessional consultations over this last complication in Hester's own affairs. How those good women there talked and talked, without ever coming one whit nearer an answer to the questions they propounded! Aunt Pepperfield wrote to them daily, and Hester occasionally, when she could spare time from her husband.

"How can Hester go on practising here, and Mr. Craig go on editing a paper there, and they not be separated?" was a question Granty put a dozen times a day.

Dorothy would answer, "Probably she will leave

practice here, and go into it there, where she can be with him."

"But she cannot take her uncle Jack's patients with her."

"No. But the sick, like the poor, are everywhere."

Again, Granty would argue for an hour, to show the inconvenience of a woman with a profession marrying a man with another, saying it ought not so to be. It *was;* and, as a remedy, Dorothy would suggest a divorce, knowing perfectly well how wicked Granty would find that proposition.

More than once Dorothy would be awakened by a voice in the quiet midnight hours. It issued from a form in shadow— garments at the footboard of the bed.

"What is it, Granty? Can't you go to sleep?"

"I don't wish to disturb you, Dorothy; but Mrs. Wickham says she is all out of pepsin and bismuth. I think Hester ought to know it, and come home, or do something."

"Let her get what she needs of Dr. Thomas."

"So she can: I did not think of that. But how is this matter going to end, Dorothy?"

"I have no idea."

"Hester was drawn into it, as you might say. She supposed he was going to die."

"But she can't kill him, now he is getting well. She does not want to, either."

"So you think she cares something about him?"

"Granty, Hester never would have married a man that she did not love, even if he had but five minutes to live. Now do go back to your rest."

Like a small but venerable spectre, Granty would vanish, only to re-appear, and suggest, in a tone half aggrieved, half suspicious, "I always supposed it was Marion that Mr. Craig had in his mind; but Hester is a very good plain cook. What would you think would be the best thing to advise, under the circumstances, Dorothy?"

"It is not of the least use for us to say. I only know that Hester has always done as she thought best, ever since she came out of her cradle, and she probably will until she goes into her grave. And you know, too, that, when she loves any one, she will cling to that one while there is any life left in her. She will do it in this case, I have no doubt. Now, please go to sleep. You will feel badly to-morrow, if you do not."

"Yes, yes, dear! in a minute. Well, I hope it will turn out all right. She is her uncle Jack right over. He always took his own way; but it seemed to be the best for others, after all."

There was a meditative silence; then just one

more remark from the good old lady, and the voices of the night were stilled. "Dorothy, things being as they are with Mr. Craig and Hester, I should say they must do as they can. I don't recollect any case like this in New England."

www.ingramcontent.com/pod-product-compliance
Lightning Source LLC
Chambersburg PA
CBHW022055230426
43672CB00008B/1184